Kingston Hotel
CAFE COOKBOOK

Kingston Hotel CAFE COOKBOOK

Free-Spirited Recipes to Warm the Soul

JUDITH WEINSTOCK

SASQUATCH BOOKS
SEATTLE

Printed in the United States of America.
Distributed in Canada by Raincoast Books Ltd.
02 01 00 99 98   5 4 3 2 1

Cover and interior design: Karen Schober
Cover and interior illustrations: Cyclone Design
Composition: Kate Basart
Copy editor: Alice Copp Smith
Indexer: Nanette Gordon

Library of Congress Cataloging-in-Publication Data
The Kingston Hotel Cafe cookbook : free-spirited recipes to warm the soul / Judith Weinstock
            p.   cm.
        Includes index.
        ISBN 1-57061-114-9 (alk.paper)
        1. Cookery, American—Pacific Northwest style. 2. Kingston Hotel Cafe (Wash.)
I. Weinstock, Judith, 1958-   . II. Kingston Hotel Cafe (Wash.)
TX715.2.P32K56   1998
641.5979—dc21   98-26357
                                                           CIP

Sasquatch Books
615 Second Avenue
Seattle, Washington 98104
(206) 467-4300
books@SasquatchBooks.com
http://www.SasquatchBooks.com

Sasquatch Books publishes high-quality adult nonfiction and children's books related to the
Northwest (Alaska to San Francisco). For more information about our titles, contact us at the
address above, or view our site on the World Wide Web.

Dedication

I dedicate this book to my parents,

Pat and Bob, who fed me a soulful diet of love, art, community,

hard work, and an appreciation for the good earth that provides for us.

And to my husband, David, for standing by me

with his feet firmly on the ground.

Acknowledgments

In acknowledgment that any endeavor dreamed

up to feed the needs of a community takes a community to create it,

I thank everyone who has participated in the success of the cafe,

through their friendship, art, humor, enjoyment, work, thought,

vision, need, desire, hope, dreams, and struggles.

CONTENTS

RECIPE LIST

Autumn

RECIPE LIST

Winter

RECIPE LIST

Spring

RECIPE LIST

Summer

INTRODUCTION

HAVING NEVER SPENT MUCH TIME buying and reading cookbooks, or feeling particularly compelled to pick up the ones given to me, I am surprised to find myself writing another one. Surprised because I came by cooking in the same way I came by breathing: I was born into it. When your umbilical cord is cut, you inhale. When you share a table with eight siblings, all reaching for the same dish, you not only inhale (the food as well as the air), you also learn how to fend for yourself. In the kitchen, I discovered I could taste food to my heart's delight without any competition and enjoy the special ingredients my mother would sometimes buy before they all disappeared. I learned how to cook out of instinct; to my young mind, cooking meant first choice and survival!

My parents had an attraction, rare for their time, to esoteric interests, including macrobiotics, a diet and philosophy rooted in Japanese tradition. But brown rice, beans, and miso were not all that attractive to us children (especially when all of our young friends were eating potato chips and Ding Dongs). We often found ourselves taking some awfully strange lunches to school. Over time, though, we came to enjoy being different. More important, the high esteem given to thoughtful preparation of food became the foundation for my growing up.

As we explored the world of macrobiotics, our family simultaneously started exploring the Cascade and Olympic mountain ranges that were near our home. Now that I am a mom myself, with two active children, I find it difficult to comprehend how my mother and father got any enjoyment out of family camping. My mother would carry the youngest child in a backpack, plus whatever else she could handle. Each child carried his or her own sleeping bag and clothes, moaning the entire way, with many interjections of "Can we stop now?" But the biggest challenge was carrying all the pots, pans, whole grains, and beans necessary for cooking macrobiotically on the trail. My father would pack up a cast-iron skillet, a stainless steel pressure cooker, his clothes and sleeping bag, sometimes a tent, and all of the food needed for nine people. (And mind you, none of the food was REI-style prepackaged, dehydrated, or *light*.) With my father's pack probably weighing in at 70 or 80 pounds and with (at that time) seven little children complaining behind him the entire way, it is a wonder we did it at all, let alone so often.

My mother and father wisely understood, though, the freedom that the Northwest woods and beaches provided for all of the family. There was enough space for us to spread out and breathe without being on top of each other. The smells, sounds, and tastes of those rich landscapes all linger in my memory: the comfort of old trees; the smell of damp roots; the light touch of ocean spray; romping with my sisters and brothers through the woods; a delicious, perfectly cooked pot of brown rice in the wilderness; my mother's homemade tofu and *seitan* (a vegetarian "meatball" made out of whole wheat dough, steamed for a long time in a soy-and-sea-vegetable marinade). With all of these memories inside of me, I will never go hungry.

I grew up, then, with an appreciation for my surroundings that was indelibly connected to my appreciation of the food I put in my mouth. The minute details and careful labor put into the preparation of macrobiotic foods—the politics of organic farming, the precise angles at which to cut vegetables to bring out their full flavor, the direction in which to stir the grain or seed when toasting—contain a certain artistry, a connection to the earth in their very language. Although I spent my early adulthood inhaling cheesecake, chocolate, and all the other foods I was not allowed to have as a child, I now find in myself a renewed personal affinity for the simplicity of whole grains, beans, and vegetables.

Although I continue to respect the diet and the philosophy, I am no longer macrobiotic. I like being open to tasting (almost!) anything. I like learning how to use new ingredients of which I've never before heard. I live for the pure joy I feel when something new bursts on my palate with a bold greeting, such as the first time I tasted the combination of oysters with Coconut-Curry-Lime Sauce (page 103) and Pineapple-Lime Salsa (page 139), or when some sensual dish beckons me to take another bite, such as Fresh Fig and Montrachet Omelet with Fig Purée (page 50).

As my older sisters and I grew into teenagers, our house became the chosen gathering place for all of our friends—who even liked our food, as long as we could sneak out to Dick's every once in a while for fishburgers. Our dinner table swelled to fit all the family—now nine children—plus all of our friends, and any other misfits that my mother so beautifully folded into the wave of ever-growing "family." Mealtimes such as these were when I experienced most acutely that I belonged to something larger, both literally and figuratively. Over time, through the relationships and security represented by all those people who joined us at our table, I found my place in the world just by feeling connected. The sharing of meals was, and is, an eminently practical and graceful way to keep that grounded feeling alive.

I like to call that sense of connection "the good life." To me, that term embraces meaningful work, being outdoors, taking care of and moving our bodies, smelling the air, enjoying each other's company, and, of course, eating good food. One of our family's recurring group epiphanies is the realization that we cannot gather in the same room for more than ten minutes before we are chronicling the last delicious meal we experienced, or describing some sweet treat that slipped into our mouths recently. Eyes light up, voices become higher and louder, hands float through the air accentuating words, and suddenly we all roll on the floor in laughter, realizing that we are at it again. Yes, we *do* enjoy good food. But it is not *just* the food. The sharing of our enjoyment of what we tasted gives us as much pleasure as the food itself.

Before she entered her macrobiotic phase, my mother, June Cleaver–style, baked huge batches of bread, half of which disappeared in the first ten minutes out of the oven. Watching her knead the bread, seeing it rise, and smelling it baking were all at least half the experience. At an early age I was already beginning to understand that food nourishes more than the belly. Food and gathering are, and always have been, the context for all of life's important rituals—birth, death, marriage, graduation, anniversaries, solace, and celebrations.

My early ventures into the kitchen are a source of comic relief now. My first baked good was an attempt to copy a friend's Ritz crackers, which I dearly coveted. My macrobiotic version was to mix some rolled oats and miso with oil, pat them as thin as I could, and bake them. As you can imagine, they weren't so great. But I quickly got better. My mother started to teach cooking classes, and by the end of them, I was her model vegetable chopper. (As a matter of fact, my speed and accuracy are a source of contention in the cafe, because along with speed comes noise. I take my moments of satisfaction sparingly, however, making sure I don't chop so often that my coworkers refuse me any pleasure at all.)

Continued forays into the kitchen expanded my already rich sense of food. After traveling and cooking on the East Coast and in Europe, I returned to Seattle to become a partner in a large collective that included Pike Place Market's Soup and Salad restaurant, Little Bread Company bakery, and Community Produce warehouse, all of which were popular in their time. I left the collective after two years to go to college, where I started a small cafe to support myself; the Corner Cafe, a student-run collective on the Evergreen State College campus, still exists as of this writing.

Upon graduating I returned to Bainbridge Island, where I had been living off and on for four years. I got a job at the new Streamliner Diner, and within a few years I bought it with three other women who had worked there. The diner was a wonderful experience but exhausting for all of us, and when we sold it in 1991, I told my husband "never again!" Then, wandering through the small community of Kingston one day a couple years later, I spotted the charming Kingston Hotel—empty and with a "For Lease" sign in the window.

So I opened the Kingston Hotel Cafe, housed in this 100-year-old Western-front building overlooking Puget Sound, the Cascade Mountain range, and Mount Rainier. It sits on a corner lot, facing east, with wide two-story front porches and high wooden fences surrounding a hidden courtyard and gardens. The café has come to feel like my family, with all of the complications and joys that come along with familial relationships—we work hard, share a lot of ourselves throughout the daily chores, and help buoy each other when our spirits are low. Over the years our relationships have deepened and work and life have integrated into a lovely collage where pieces of all of our worlds overlap. This venue for my livelihood has felt quite natural and fulfilling.

I now begin each day at the Kingston Hotel Cafe with rituals that are as much a part of the outcome of a given dish or meal as the ingredients themselves. Most days, I begin with time outside. The changing of the seasons, the smell of the air, the color of the sky, the planting of seeds in spring and putting to rest of beds in winter, the spray of the water each day as I run on the beach—these are the fundamental ingredients that enable me to begin cooking. Everywhere I turn in my corner of the Puget Sound country there is the undeniable link of survival and rejuvenation within the earth, the air, and the water, and within the growing and preparation of food. Thus, eating and the enjoyment thereof become not just a physical necessity but a soulful enactment of life itself. This, ultimately, is my recipe for entering the cafe's kitchen.

Seasonal cooking in the Pacific Northwest is an amalgamation rich beyond my wildest dreams. Our native bounty is renowned and beloved: Northwest seafood, summer berries, wild mushrooms, superb fruits and vegetables. And, because our Pacific Rim location lets us import fanciful ingredients from all over the world, the kitchen becomes a Disneyesque playground, where anything you dream up, you can have at your fingertips. I have been heard to say (more than once) that the only reason I have gone through the agony of four restaurants is because I can "play" to my heart's content, and buy ingredients I could never afford at home, with a reasonable excuse: I must please the customers. It is a win-win situation.

Going into the kitchen playfully is not only important to me, it is the reason I cook. I seldom say no to an idea—which is a source of much humor in the cafe's kitchen. On the wall we have a cartoon quote about "pizza with hollandaise sauce topped with sushi" and I agree that the whole idea of "fusion" food has gone too far. But in the cafe, an instinctive overlap of ingredients or ideas occurs with, most of the time, grand results. I will be staring into a pot of carrot soup, looking at the beautiful orange color, and bingo! I realize that oranges would taste good with carrots. The oranges get zested and juiced, and as I'm adding them, one more flavor pops into my head—fennel. Daily, ever-broader flavor marriages are born from this sense of play.

I liken the cooking process to learning music. Once you understand the mathematical principles that tie the notes together, you can begin to play with the forms and apply the rules to any instrument. Likewise, by attaining a firm understanding of flavors, combinations, textures, and timing, you can follow your own rules with food. This is when cooking really becomes fun.

So, if you are inclined, look for parallels in the recipes, ingredient combinations, and processes in this book. For instance, the idea of a roulade is to roll something up in meat. I had so much fun rolling cheeses, herbs, and vegetables in thin fillets of fish or meat, it suddenly hit me one day that I could roll similar ingredients in bread. And voilà!

In my insecure moments, I think all of this will prove I have no real talent. I'm just doing the same thing over and over again, with a little variation. But then I think perhaps this is what it means to be creative: to do a million variations on the same theme and to let the mind take an idea to its limit. And when I am happily cooking, I don't think about it at all. I am enjoying the moment. I hope this collection of recipes inspires you to create, and brings you some good moments of your own.

Judith Weinstock
Kingston, Washington

A Well-Stocked Kitchen

ALTHOUGH MANY PANTRY LISTS are comprised simply of dry goods and non-perishable items, there are plenty of perishable ingredients that are elemental to fresh, seaonal cooking. For instance, I always have on hand gingerroot and citrus, which play a part in dozens of the cafe's recipes throughout the year—from breads or soups to seafood or salsa. I use such items often enough, and they keep for long enough periods, that they have become standard ingredients with which I stock my kitchen. Here, I've listed the basics that I always like to have around, regardless of what type of cooking I'm doing. Note that some of the items are limited by the season in which they are available.

STAPLES

beans (black, pinto, azuki, kidney)

corn masa (white and blue)

flours (unbleached white, fine and coarse whole wheat, semolina, buckwheat, corn, rye)

lentils

pastas (semolina, rice, bean threads, soba)

polenta (fine, medium, coarse)

rices (jasmine, basmati, arborio, sushi)

split peas

SOUPS AND STOCKS

all spices

bay leaves

canola oil

dried mushrooms and/or mushroom powder (shiitake, porcini, morels)

good olive oil

good soy sauce (such as Tamari brand or other wheat free)

sea vegetables (arame, kombu, wakame, nori)

seasoned rice vinegar

whole chickens

QUICK ADDITIONS AND ACCENTS

canned beans (cannellini garbanzo, navy)

canned green chiles

canned Roma tomatoes

capers

chili oil

coconut milk

cooking wines and liqueurs (Triple Sec, Pernod, brandy, rum, sherry, port, marsala)

fish sauce

nuts (almonds, pecans, cashews, peanuts, hazelnuts)

sesame seeds (white, black, brown)

sweeteners (honey, maple syrup, molasses, brown and granulated sugar)

tahini

tamarind paste

toasted sesame oil

vinegars (apple cider, red wine, white wine, rice, floral, herbal)

wasabi powder

Worcestershire sauce

FROM THE GARDEN

avocados

baby dill

basil

bell peppers (various colors)

carrots

celery

cilantro

cucumbers

eggplant

garlic

gingerroot

hot peppers (sweet, jalapeño, serrano, Anaheim, specialty)

lemons

limes

onions (shallots, chives, green, yellow sweet, purple)

oranges

oregano

parsley

potatoes

Roma tomatoes

salad greens

seasonal squash

tarragon

DAIRY

butter (salted and unsalted)

buttermilk

cheeses (fresh mozzarella, good sharp white Cheddar, Gruyère, Brie, Montrachet, Parmigiano-Reggiano, pecorino Romano, feta, Asiago, ricotta)

cream★

eggs

milk (whole and nonfat)

sour cream

★Some of the recipes in this book use heavy cream. At home I rarely cook with heavy cream, and so I substitute like this:

1 cup heavy cream =
⅔ cup good yogurt + ⅓ cup milk
or
¾ cup nonfat yogurt + ¼ cup nonfat milk
(my father-in-law can't have any fat because of heart problems)
or
⅓ cup steamed and puréed potatoes + ⅔ cup milk

These substitutions will vary depending on the quality of the yogurt, milk, and potatoes. Cream quality can vary a great deal as well. Legally a whipping cream only has to be about 24% butterfat, but the really good ones are about 48%! That is a major difference for a recipe. So, when you are substituting, compare taste, and adjust accordingly.

You can use these substitutions for any recipe in this book. You will need to adjust seasonings a bit sometimes, because of the slight variations in flavor (yogurt is a little tart, while potatoes are not, for example). Thus, a tiny bit of salt (literally maybe only a pinch) or honey (½ teaspoon) may be needed for the perfect balance.

Sauces, Salsas, Chutneys & More
Serving Suggestions

Recipe	Paired with Kingston Hotel Cafe Dishes	General Serving Tips	Storage
Ancho Chile–Tamarind Sauce, 33		Use as a dipping sauce; as an alternative to sour cream; on top of eggs, chicken, pork, and rice; as an addition to other sauces	Will keep in a tightly lidded container in the refrigerator for up to 1 week
Avocado–Pumpkin Seed Salsa, 55	Mexican Fish Cakes, 54	Use as a salsa or specialty guacamole	Serve immediately
Balsamic and Mustard Vinaigrette, 9		Serve on green salads	Will keep in a tightly lidded container in the refrigerator for up to 1 month
Cafe Roma Tomato Sauce, 75		Use as a sauce for pasta and pizza; under polenta; for poaching fish; for baking eggs	Will keep in a tightly lidded container in the refrigerator for up to 1 week
Cafe Secret Sauce, 76	Fresh Soba Noodles with Burdock Root, Ginger, and Wild Greens, 67 Ahi Tuna Cakes with Green Onion, Sesame, and Ginger, 107 Parsnip-Coconut Cakes with Seared Salmon, 108	Use as a marinade for vegetables, seafood, and meat (especially when grilling); for searing meat and seafood; as a salad dressing for soba noodle and rice salads	Will keep in a tightly lidded container in the refrigerator for up to 3 weeks
Cafe Ten-Spice Marinade, 69	Cafe Ten-Spice Chicken Sauté, 68	Use as a marinade for chicken, fish, and pork; for searing meat, poultry, and fish; in rice dishes; (Uses are similar to those for the Cafe Secret Sauce, see above)	Will keep in a tightly lidded container in the refrigerator for up to 2 weeks
Citrus–Ancho Chile Sauce, 140		Serve over omelets filled with spicy sausage, onion, and Cheddar cheese; with lunch burritos filled with chicken, chiles, and cheese; with prawns and Mexican rice; with any dish of eggs, chicken, fish, or tamales	Will keep in a tightly lidded container in the refrigerator for up to 2 weeks

Sauces, Salsas, Chutneys & More
Serving Suggestions

Recipe	Paired with Kingston Hotel Cafe Dishes	General Serving Tips	Storage
Coconut-Curry-Lime Sauce, 103	Risotto with Rock Shrimp and Spinach, 102 Curried Oyster Scramble with Papaya-Mango Salsa, 6	Use with seafood, rice dishes, risotto, and pasta dishes (Asian rice noodles especially)	Will keep in a tightly lidded container in the refrigerator for up to 3 days
Cool As a Cucumber Raita, 142	Ahi Tuna Cakes with Green Onion, Sesame, and Ginger, 107 Mexican Fish Cakes, 54 Pakistani Homefries, 88	Serve with fish cakes, potatoes, and rice dishes	Serve immediately
Cran-Tequila Sauce, 77		Serve with smoked trout or a grilled dense white fish such as halibut; use as a sauce for roasted turkey	Will keep in a tightly lidded container in the refrigerator for up to 2 weeks
Cranberry-Orange Sauce and Relish, 30	Sweet Potato Blintzes, 8 Sourdough Waffles, 122	Serve with poultry (especially turkey and duck breast), seafood, and smoked trout	The sauce will keep in a tightly lidded container in the refrigerator for up to 2 weeks and the relish will keep for up to 1 week
Fig Purée, 51	Fresh Fig and Montrachet Omelet, 50	Serve with waffles, ravioli, or duck	Will keep in a tightly lidded container in the refrigerator for up to 2 weeks
Fresh Ginger–Curry Vinaigrette, 137	Wild Green Salad with Spiced Nuts, Pear, Montrachet, and Mango, 131	Serve with couscous or rice salads that have an Eastern or Asian flavor	Will keep in a tightly lidded container in the refrigerator for up to 1 month
Lemony Sorrel and Spinach Sauce, 109		Serve with poached salmon; over rice; on bread; for dipping vegetables	Will keep in a tightly lidded container in the refrigerator for up to 1 week
Mango Chutney, 138	Steamed Halibut in Spicy Yogurt Sauce, 27 Indian Halibut Cakes, 121	Serve with "rice table" meals, seafood, poultry, salads, and meats; as a condiment; in dressings	This chutney will keep in a tightly lidded container in the refrigerator for up to 1 month
Orange Blossom Dressing, 141	Serve over a spinach salad with tropical fruit (mango or papaya) and Spiced Nuts, 68 Over a light beet salad	Use as a garnish for soups such as butternut squash; for dipping vegetables	Will keep in a tightly lidded container in the refrigerator for up to 2 weeks

Sauces, Salsas, Chutneys & More
Serving Suggestions

Recipe	Paired with Kingston Hotel Cafe Dishes	General Serving Tips	Storage
Orange-Cinnamon-Curry Dressing, 110	Couscous Salad, 106	Serve over green salads, rice salads, and couscous salads	Will keep in a tightly lidded container in the refrigerator for up to 2 weeks
Papaya-Mango Salsa, 7	Curried Oyster Scramble, 6 Fresh Yellowfin Tuna Cakes, 132	Serve with poultry, seafood, rice dishes, egg dishes, or salads	Serve immediately
Papaya–Red Pepper Salsa, 112		Serve with oysters, bean and rice platters, halibut, scallops, and frittatas	Serve immediately
Pear-Ginger Sauce, 53	Buckwheat Cinnamon Waffles, 52	Serve over waffles and omelets; with pork and chicken	Will keep in a tightly lidded container in the refrigerator for 7–10 days
Pineapple-Lime Salsa, 139	Mexican Fish Cakes, 54 Fresh Yellowfin Tuna Cakes, 132	Serve with eggs, fish cakes, and grilled tuna; on soups	Serve immediately
Quince Purée, 15	Sweet Potato and Spice Pancakes, 14 Sweet Potato Blintzes, 8 Buckwheat Crepes, 16	Use as an alternative to applesauce Serve on top of waffles; in cobblers; with potato pancakes	Will keep in a tightly lidded container in the refrigerator for up to 1 week
Roasted Tomatillo–Green Pepper Sauce, 34		Serve on top of burritos; under grilled fish; over eggs; tossed with noodles	Will keep in a tightly lidded container in the refrigerator for up to 1 week
Savory Carrot-Thyme Tomato Sauce, 32	Fettucine with Walnuts, Asiago, and Spinach, 23 Halibut Roulades, 29 Confetti Ravioli with Carrot and Basil, 72	Use as a sauce for pizza, pasta, seafood, and poultry	Will keep in a tightly lidded container in the refrigerator for up to 1 week
Spiced Plum Sauce, 11	Corn Waffles, 10 Sourdough Waffles, 122 Confetti Ravioli with Carrot and Basil, 72	Serve with ravioli or poultry (such as duck or chicken); over omelets	Will keep in a tightly lidded container in the refrigerator for 7–10 days

Sauces, Salsas, Chutneys & More
Serving Suggestions

Recipe	Paired with Kingston Hotel Cafe Dishes	General Serving Tips	Storage
Spicy Green Apple–Tequila Sauce, 65	Seared Pork Tenderloin, 64 White Cheddar and Green Chile Tamales, 66 Spicy Ancho Chile and Fresh Mozzarella Tamales, 28 Potato-Tarragon Pancakes, 94	Serve with dense white fish, poultry, pork, and tamales	Will keep in a tightly lidded container in the refrigerator for 7–10 days
Summer Strawberry Salsa, 143	Pear-Ginger Soup, 97 Chilled Peach Soup, 128	Use as a garnish for chilled fruit soups; serve with fish cakes	Serve immediately
Two-Squash Salsa, 111	Lentil-Tomato Harvest Soup, 19 Black Bean, Lime, and Chile Soup, 60 Spicy Ancho Chile and Fresh Mozzarella Tamales, 28 Smoked Salmon–Corn Cakes, 85	Use as a garnish for soups; as a topping for summer frittatas Serve with rice dishes, fish, eggs, chicken, blackened fish, or summer rice dishes	Serve immediately, or cover, refrigerate, and use within 24 hours

Dessert Accents
Serving Suggestions

Recipe	Paired with Kingston Hotel Cafe Dishes	General Serving Tips	Storage
Chocolate Cream Glaze, 39	Chocolate Mousse Cake, 36	Serve on ice cream; over pies; in espresso drinks Use as filling and glaze for cakes; for dipping strawberries	Will keep in a tightly lidded container in the refrigerator for up to 2 weeks
Chocolate Rum Buttercream, 42	Hazelnut Torte, 40	Use as filling and icing for chocolate or white cake	Serve immediately
Cinnamon Cream, 11	Corn Waffles, 10	Serve in a coffee or a mocha; on waffles; with apple pie; over cake	Serve immediately
Lemon Curd, 145	Orange Blossom Cake, 144	Use as a thin layer in cakes, fruit tarts, and cheesecakes	Will keep in a tightly lidded container in the refrigerator for up to 1 month
Vanilla Buttercream, 38	Chocolate Mousse Cake, 36	Use as a filling and icing for cake	Best on first day, but can be frozen and re-whipped after being brought back to room temperature

AUTUMN

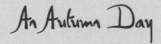

An Autumn Day

BREAKFAST:
Corn Waffles with Spiced Plum Sauce and Cinnamon Cream

LUNCH:
Cafe Pizza with caramelized onions, portobello mushrooms,
Montrachet cheese, fresh herbs, and high-quality olive oil

DINNER:
Shiitake–Orange Blossom Soup, Four Mushroom Risotto

AuTuMn

— —

MY NOSE GREETS AUTUMN FIRST. Early fall days often look like summer outside, but as soon as I open the door I can smell the change of season. Throughout my childhood this experience always seemed to coincide with the first day of school. We were pulled from our long summer slumber, dressed, fed, and—still half asleep— guided out the door. By the time I reached the end of the driveway I was fully awake; school and autumn greeted me together, with a bit of sternness, excitement and chill. By midafternoon, though, the sun would return—a moment of summer respite, gently moving us toward the new season. Autumn lets us down easy in the Pacific Northwest.

In the cafe kitchen, autumnal excitement comes to its height with the magical appearance of Northwest mushrooms: shaggy mane, matsutake, chanterelle, oyster, lion's mane, and more push through the earth with the first fall rains. Those who spend time in search of these delectable morsels conceal their locations like a child with hidden treasure. Each mushroom has its own distinctive flavor and its own culinary enthusiasts. Like our berry-mania in summer, mushrooms pop up in our dishes as abundantly as they appear on the forest floor after a rain. We might fill an herb sourdough with Gruyère and mushrooms for brunch, and then sauté risotto with lots of garlic, parsley, Romano, and our favorite fungi for dinner. Open-face grilled mushroom sandwiches appear on the lunch board, and every kind of mushroom soup is dreamed up, our favorite being an aromatic, sensuous marriage of orange-flower water and shiitake mushrooms.

I think of autumn as the "root and vine" season. I start burrowing into my archives of potato recipes; beet, carrot, and parsnip recipe ideas follow closely behind. Then I am pulled back into the sunnier domain of Indian-summer corns and pumpkins.

The cafe's garden at this time is still in full bloom, but lunch or dinner among the lush greenery is sometimes hindered by heavy breezes, gray skies, and the sudden onslaught of cool rain. In between these moments, the sky is deep blue and steam rises off the tables. As in the tropics, every leaf reaches toward the light, steamy, wet, and warm, magnified by drops of water reflecting little rainbows. This is a magical time to enjoy a meal in the garden—but be prepared to move inside at a moment's notice!

Comice Pear and Montrachet Omelet

I am so drawn to the flavors of pear and Montrachet that I put them on pizza, fold them into omelets, and toss them in salads. The combination of the sweet, crisp pear and the smooth, creamy Montrachet sits in perfect camaraderie on your tongue. I top this omelet with a pear purée.

In a small skillet on medium-high heat, sauté the garlic and onion in 1 teaspoon of the butter or oil until the onion becomes transparent. Add the pear and stir. Add the wine, sugar, and salt. Cook a minute or two more just so that the flavors combine. Set aside.

Place the other teaspoon of butter or oil in an omelet pan on medium heat. When it is just melted, pour the beaten eggs into the pan, making sure they cover the entire bottom. When they have set, flip the omelet and turn the heat off. Cover half of the omelet with the Montrachet and the sautéed pear mixture. Flip the other half over the filling and serve the omelet topped with a pear purée.

Yield: 1 serving

½ teaspoon minced garlic

¼ cup finely diced onion

2 teaspoons butter or canola oil

¼ cup unpeeled and diced Comice pear

Splash of muscat canelli

Pinch of sugar

Pinch of salt

3 large eggs, beaten

2 tablespoons Montrachet cheese

Pear purée (see Note on p. 53)

Curried Oyster Scramble with Papaya-Mango Salsa

*The first time I ever ate oysters I was 15, on a sailing trip in the San Juan Islands.
We sailed into a cove, looking for a spot to set up tents for the night. As we gazed down
into the depths of the water, we realized that the mottled colors on the bottom didn't make
sense with how the sand and rocks usually look. We reached down to investigate further and
started pulling up oysters by the dozen. The cove bottom was covered with oysters! We filled
the bottom of the little 17-foot Poulsbo Queen and had a feast that night. My sister
Jill even found some pearls! Needless to say, I ate too many oysters, and I had
not been able to eat them since—until I put this recipe together.*

1 teaspoon minced garlic

2 green onions, chopped

¼ cup finely diced red bell pepper

1 tablespoon canola oil

⅓ cup roughly chopped spinach leaves, packed

¼ cup Coconut-Curry-Lime Sauce (p. 103)

5 small fresh oysters

3 eggs, beaten

Salt and pepper

Papaya-Mango Salsa (recipe follows)

In a medium-sized, smooth-bottomed pan on medium-high heat, sauté the garlic, green onions, and red pepper in the oil until the pepper softens a little. Add the spinach and the Coconut-Curry-Lime Sauce. Turn the heat to low and cover the pan. When the spinach has wilted, turn the heat back up, add the oysters, and lightly poach for 4–5 minutes, until the oysters plump. You may need a little more of the curry sauce, depending on how juicy the oysters are and how much evaporates when cooking. Add eggs, salt, and pepper and stir until eggs are cooked through. Serve with a dollop of Papaya-Mango Salsa.

Yield: 1 serving

Papaya-Mango Salsa

*Fruit salsas have become such a part of my diet and of the cafe menu—
breakfast, lunch, and dinner—that I find it difficult to imagine anyplace where they
wouldn't fit in. I use this one with the Curried Oyster Scramble (preceding page), with any
poultry, seafood, rice dishes, or egg dishes, and even with salads!*

Mix all ingredients together. This sauce is best served immediately. The cilantro wilts and loses its freshness if it sits too long.

Note: Substitute strawberries for the papaya and find yourself submerged in a tropical dream come true—I served this variation with ahi tuna at the cafe on Valentine's Day.

Yield: About 3½ cups

1½ cups finely diced papaya

1 cup finely diced mango

1 cup finely diced pineapple

¼ cup minced red bell pepper

½ teaspoon minced fresh jalapeño pepper

½ cup roughly chopped cilantro leaves

Zest and juice of 2 limes

1 teaspoon salt

4 teaspoons sugar

Sweet Potato Blintzes

A blintz is a crepe that is stuffed, traditionally with a filling of sweetened ricotta or other soft cheese. At the cafe I serve these with Quince Purée (p. 15), Cranberry-Orange Sauce (p. 30), or applesauce, depending on the season and what is available.

CREPES:

3 eggs, beaten

1⅓ cups milk

2 tablespoons butter, melted and cooled slightly

¾ cup unbleached white flour

½ teaspoon salt

Canola oil for cooking the unfilled crepes

FILLING:

½ cup currants

¼ cup brandy

2⅔ cups cooked sweet potato

1 cup cream cheese, at room temperature

Zest of 1 lemon

1¼ teaspoons cinnamon

2 tablespoons honey or sugar

Butter or canola oil for frying the filled crepes

For the crepes: In a medium-sized bowl with a whisk, or in a food processor, blend the eggs, milk, and melted butter. Add the flour and salt and briskly whisk or blend until creamy in texture. Cover and refrigerate for 1 hour.

On medium heat, pour ¼ cup of batter at a time into a lightly oiled pan, tilting the pan to spread the batter evenly over the bottom. Let cook until the edges pull away from the sides of the pan. Flip. Let cook 10–15 more seconds on the other side. Remove to a plate. Repeat the process until all of the batter is used. Stack the crepes and cover until you are ready to fill or use.

For the filling: Soak currants in brandy for 30 minutes. In a medium-sized bowl, mash together all of the filling ingredients.

Spoon approximately ⅓ cup of the filling into the middle of each crepe. Fold the two sides of the crepe over the filling, then fold in the top and the bottom. On medium heat, with a little butter or canola oil, fry the blintzes in a heavy-bottomed skillet until golden brown on both sides. Serve immediately.

Note: I sometimes make these blintzes with pumpkin or butternut squash instead of sweet potatoes. Any of these are delicious. You will need to adjust the amounts of sweetener and cream cheese a little, depending on which you use (sweet potatoes and butternut squash are generally much sweeter than pumpkin).

Storage: You can refrigerate crepes after they are made, for up to 4 days, or freeze them for up to a month. If you freeze them, place sheets of waxed paper between them as you stack them.

Yield: 5 servings (10 crepes)

BALSAMIC AND MUSTARD VINAIGRETTE

This is our house dressing. We use it on all of our dinner and green salads.

½ cup balsamic vinegar
½ cup seasoned rice vinegar
1 tablespoon coarse mustard
2 teaspoons dried basil
1 teaspoon dried thyme

1 teaspoon dried oregano
1 tablespoon minced fresh garlic
1 teaspoon salt
1 ½ cups olive oil

In a blender or food processor, blend all ingredients except the oil for 1 minute. With the food processor still running, pour in the oil in a thin stream until it is fully combined.

Storage: This dressing will keep in a tightly lidded container in the refrigerator for up to 1 month.

Yield: About 2½ cups

Corn Waffles with Spiced Plum Sauce and Cinnamon Cream

*Just the name of this recipe wakens my taste buds into an excited frenzy!
Come the end of summer, I get phone calls from a number of friends asking me
to join them to gather all of the fallen, unharvested plums off the ground. I ready
my kitchen to can whole plums, plum chutney, and plum sauce, and by the
end of the day visions of sugar plums are dancing in my head.*

*Although corn and plums are both in full harvest at the beginning of autumn,
I can't deny myself the complete satisfaction of serving this dish on Christmas morning.*

---

3 cups unbleached white flour

2 cups cornmeal

5 teaspoons baking powder

1 tablespoon baking soda

1 teaspoon salt

7 large eggs, separated

½ pound (2 sticks) butter or margarine, melted and slightly cooled

4 cups buttermilk

Zest of 1 orange

Spiced Plum Sauce (recipe follows)

Cinnamon Cream (recipe follows)

Heat the waffle iron.

Sift together the flour, cornmeal, baking powder, baking soda, and salt into a large mixing bowl.

In a separate bowl, beat the egg whites until they form stiff peaks.

In still another large mixing bowl, whisk the egg yolks until they turn a light yellow. While continuing to whisk, add the melted butter, buttermilk, and orange zest.

With a large spoon or spatula, stir the dry ingredients into the wet ingredients until they are fully incorporated. Fold in the egg whites.

Grease the waffle iron. Pour ¾ cup batter for each waffle onto the waffle iron and cook for about 3 minutes.

Serve with Spiced Plum Sauce and Cinnamon Cream.

Yield: Seven 7-inch waffles

Spiced Plum Sauce

*Try filling an omelet with a light goat cheese such as Montrachet, then
top it with this sauce. Dessert for breakfast! I have also served this sauce on Sourdough
Waffles (p. 122), with ravioli, and with poultry such as duck or chicken.*

In a medium-sized pot, bring the plums, water, and sugar to a boil. Lower heat and simmer for ½ hour, or until the plums have completely broken down. Purée until smooth in a blender or food processor. Whisk in the rest of the ingredients.

Storage: This sauce will keep in a tightly lidded container in the refrigerator for 7–10 days. It will keep in the freezer for up to 1 month.

Yield: About 6 cups

8 cups Italian plums, pitted

2 cups water

1 cup sugar

Zest and juice of 2 lemons

Zest and juice of 1 orange

1 tablespoon peeled and grated fresh gingerroot

2 teaspoons cinnamon

¼ teaspoon cloves

½ teaspoon nutmeg

¼ teaspoon cardamom

½ cup port

Cinnamon Cream

*This is delicious in coffee, on waffles, in a mocha,
next to apple pie, or over cake. Try it—you'll like it!*

With an electric mixer, whip the cream and cinnamon, gradually adding the sugar or honey, until stiff.

Yield: 4 cups

1 pint heavy whipping cream

2 teaspoons cinnamon

¼ cup sugar or honey

Wild Mushroom Braid with Herbs and Gruyère

Although I usually serve this for weekend brunch, it also makes a lovely late-summer evening meal with a Caesar salad. You can use the basic idea, make the same dough, and fill it with whatever ingredients strike your fancy at the moment. I have filled it with roasted vegetables (Jerusalem artichokes, red bell peppers, and shallots), prosciutto, and Asiago cheese. I have also filled it with asparagus, ham, chèvre, and herbs. You can think of this dish as you might think of focaccia or pizza: find a combination of flavors that you like, and it will probably work.

DOUGH:

1 cup minced onion

2 tablespoons olive oil

4 cups sourdough starter (see Note, below)

2 teaspoons salt

1 tablespoon honey

1 teaspoon minced fresh thyme

1½ teaspoons minced fresh marjoram

2 tablespoons chopped chives

5 cups unbleached white flour plus additional as needed

FILLING:

1 tablespoon minced garlic

1½ cups minced onion

1 tablespoon butter or olive oil

2 cups sliced shiitake mushrooms (or any combination of the following: chanterelle, oyster, portobello, or matsutake mushrooms)

2 cups chopped raw spinach, packed

3 tablespoons marsala

1 teaspoon chopped fresh rosemary

½ teaspoon salt

4 cups grated Gruyère cheese

1 egg, beaten, for brushing tops of braids

For the dough: In a medium-sized skillet, sauté the onion in the olive oil. Set aside to cool.

Pour the starter into a large mixing bowl. Whisk in the salt, honey, thyme, marjoram, and chives. Whisk in the sautéed onion. Add 1 cup of the flour and whisk it in until it is fully incorporated. Continue adding 1 cup of flour at a time until you can no longer use a whisk. Turn the dough out onto your work surface and knead in the rest of the flour ½ cup at a time. When all of the flour is incorporated, knead another 3 minutes. Place in a lightly oiled bowl, cover, and let rise for 45 minutes.

For the filling: In a large skillet, sauté the garlic and onion in the butter or olive oil on high heat until the onion becomes transparent. Add the mushrooms and sauté 1 minute more. Add the spinach and marsala, lower heat to medium, cover, and cook for 2–3 minutes, until the spinach has wilted. Uncover and add the rosemary and salt. Set aside.

Dust your work surface with flour. Divide the dough into two equal pieces. Roll out each piece into a long rectangle, approximately 14 x 18 inches (just make it longer than it is wide—it will shrink as it sits). Dust the surface of the rectangle with flour, and fold in half lengthwise, producing a rectangle about 7 x 18 inches. Do not press down on the dough.

With a sharp, straight-edged knife, make a row of parallel diagonal cuts, 1 inch apart, through both layers of the long nonfolded edge, cutting two thirds of the distance in toward the folded edge.

Unfold the dough, returning it to the size it was originally. The rectangle should now be divided into three parts visually. The two rows of "fingers" that you have cut each take up one third of the width of the rectangle, with the middle third being left uncut. Spread 2 cups of the grated Gruyère in the middle, uncut, area of the dough. Place half the mushroom-and-spinach mixture on top of that.

Weave the fingers, like a braid, over the filling, crossing alternately the left, then the right, then the left, then the right, until you have braided all of the fingers.

Lightly oil two 11 x 17-inch baking sheets. Place one braid on each sheet. Cover and let rise for 45 minutes in a warm place.

Preheat the oven to 375°F.

Brush the tops of the braids with the beaten egg and bake for 35–40 minutes, until the tops and bottoms are golden brown.

Note: My father-in-law loves our sourdough bread and has tried numerous times to transport some of our starter back home to New York so he can make his own. Once, he left it on the ferry. Another time, it spilled in his luggage (yuck!). When he never returned home successfully with it, he decided to ask bakeries and specialty stores in Manhattan for some starter. Although he was willing to pay for it, all declined. I had to laugh, because I try to give starter away whenever I have "grown" too much for my own use. Although I have urged it on many a customer, often I end up dumping some in the garbage. Many stores with specialty food sections or bakeries offer a sourdough starter mix. Our starter, however, is 100 years old, making its quality unsurpassed in my mind.

Yield: 2 braids

Sweet Potato and Spice Pancakes with Quince Purée

*Sweet potatoes and quinces begin to arrive about the time of year when
the morning sun through the window still looks like hot summer. You pull your
shorts on, throw on a T-shirt, and step outdoors—to a flourish of goose bumps on your
arms and legs. Suddenly you are hungry for a little more than a bowl of
fresh fruit. This breakfast keeps you feeling warm all day.*

2½ cups unbleached white flour

2¼ teaspoons baking powder

1½ teaspoons baking soda

¼ cup sugar

¾ teaspoon salt

¾ teaspoon curry powder

¾ teaspoon cinnamon

¼ teaspoon nutmeg

¼ teaspoon cloves

4 eggs

¼ pound (1 stick) butter, melted and cooled

2 cups buttermilk

Zest and juice of 1 orange

1½ teaspoons peeled and minced fresh gingerroot

1½ cups grated raw sweet potatoes, unpeeled

Oil for cooking

Quince Purée (recipe follows)

Sift together the flour, baking powder, baking soda, sugar, salt, and spices into a large bowl. Set aside.

Separate the eggs. Beat the whites until they form stiff peaks and set aside.

In another large mixing bowl, whisk the yolks until light in color. Add the melted butter, buttermilk, orange zest and juice, gingerroot, and sweet potatoes, continuing to whisk until all the ingredients are thoroughly incorporated.

Make a well in the middle of the dry ingredients. Pour the wet ingredients into the well. Stir together until the ingredients are completely incorporated. Fold in the egg whites.

On medium heat, pour ¼ cup of batter per cake into a lightly oiled skillet. Cook until the edges turn golden brown and the tops begin to bubble. Flip, and cook on the other side for 3 minutes on low heat. Serve immediately with Quince Purée.

Yield: 4–6 servings (about 10 cakes)

Quince Purée

Quince is often likened to apple in flavor. But there really is nothing quite like it. The first time I cooked some up and tasted it, I ate a whole bowlful. It was like applesauce, but better! Quinces are very hard fruits, so be sure to have a sharp knife around and a good sense of humor if you are going to make a huge amount of anything with them!

I use this purée on top of waffles, in cobblers, or with potato pancakes—anywhere you might use applesauce. The flavor is most pleasant, yet not quite identifiable because of its uniqueness.

In a medium-sized saucepan, bring the quince, wine, apple juice, and water to a boil. Lower heat and simmer, covered, for ½ hour, or until the quince has softened all the way through. Blend in a food processor or blender with the lemon zest, lemon juice, and sugar or honey until completely smooth in texture.

Storage: This purée will keep in a tightly lidded container in the refrigerator for up to 1 week.

Yield: 6 cups

8 cups cored and diced quince
1½ cups muscat canelli
2 cups apple juice
1 cup water
Zest of 2 lemons
½ cup fresh lemon juice
10 tablespoons sugar or honey

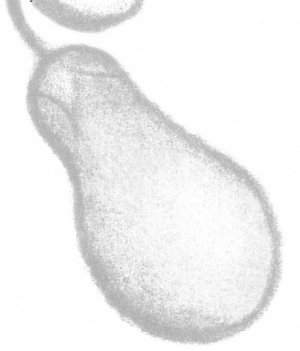

Buckwheat Crepes with Mascarpone and Blackberries

*When we tested these at the cafe, Andrea, one of our waitstaff, rolled
them up with applesauce and then with quince purée, and even slathered some
tahini and maple syrup on one. They were delicious every way.*

4 eggs, beaten

1½ cups milk

3 tablespoons melted butter

½ cup buckwheat flour

½ cup unbleached white flour

½ teaspoon cinnamon

¾ teaspoon salt

Butter for frying

1 pound mascarpone cheese

4 cups blackberries

In a medium-sized bowl, mix together the eggs, milk, and melted butter. Whisk in the flours, cinnamon, and salt until thoroughly blended. Refrigerate batter for 1 hour.

Use an 8-inch crepe pan or a smooth-bottomed omelet pan. On medium heat, brush the pan lightly with butter. Pour ¼ cup batter into the pan while tilting it to spread the batter evenly and thinly over the bottom. When the crepe begins to pull away from the pan at the edges, flip. Cook for 15 seconds more and remove from the pan. Repeat the process until all of the batter is gone. You may use the crepes immediately, or wrap them in plastic and refrigerate.

To finish the recipe, divide the mascarpone and blackberries equally among the crepes, roll, and serve.

Yield: 5–8 servings (about 15 crepes)

Parsnip-Brandy Soup with Anise

The first time I can remember tasting parsnips was on our family's cross-country journey from Seattle to Boston in the fall of '68. My parents had taken all seven children out of school, and everything we owned in the whole wide world was in our van with us. As we drove into the Southwest, I recall my first sense of being set free from the humdrum dailiness of school, and of the inherent exuberance of childhood spirit, thirsting to live in the moment. My first sights of the crimson-and-gold sunsets of the desert, with bats' strobelike wings against the neon-blue sky; black widow spiders; playing in the searing heat of the day and sleeping in the autumn cool of the nights; signs of the presence of rattlesnakes; and the pure taste of fresh water from the spring—all merged into my experience of meals cooked on the open fire in the desert.

What did my mother find at the local grocery store or produce stand that suited her discriminating dietary needs there in the Southwest? Parsnips. And now parsnips inevitably comingle with my potent memories of Mesa Verde and the Grand Canyon. They will never again occupy in my mind the lowly place of a mere vegetable.

In a medium-sized, heavy-bottomed pot, sauté the garlic and onion in the butter or oil until the onion is transparent. Add the parsnips and sauté another 3 minutes. Add the apple juice and water, cover, and bring to a boil. Turn down to simmer for 20–25 minutes, or until the parsnip falls apart when poked.

In a small, dry skillet on high heat, toast the anise seed, stirring constantly, until light brown. Grind with a mortar and pestle or in a small coffee or spice grinder.

In a food processor or blender, purée the parsnip and onion mixture until smooth. Add the lemon zest, lemon juice, anise seed, brandy, cream or yogurt, salt, and sugar. Stir. Put back on low heat for 5–10 minutes. Do not boil. Serve immediately.

1 tablespoon minced garlic

2 cups diced onion

4 tablespoons butter or canola oil

5 cups coarsely chopped parsnips

3¾ cups apple juice

1 cup water

1 teaspoon whole anise seed

Zest of 1 lemon

⅓ cup freshly squeezed lemon juice

½ cup brandy

1 cup heavy cream or yogurt

1¾ teaspoons salt

1 tablespoon sugar

Yield: 4–6 servings

Fall Pumpkin Soup with Fennel

*Because pumpkin (like potato) can carry different and strong flavors well,
I make several kinds of pumpkin soup. This one seems particularly appropriate during
Halloween season, not only because of the pumpkin but because of the fennel, which is
in the "licorice-flavored" spice category. Fennel is not overpowering to those who
do not like licorice, and it definitely adds a sweet dimension.*

3 tablespoons minced garlic

1 cup diced onion

4 cups peeled and chopped fresh sugar pumpkin

6 tablespoons canola oil

2 cups apple juice

½ teaspoon whole fennel seed

½ teaspoon whole cumin seed

1 teaspoon whole coriander seed

½ teaspoon cinnamon

¼ teaspoon cloves

Zest of 1 orange

½ cup yogurt

½ cup cream

2 tablespoons honey

2 teaspoons salt

In a heavy-bottomed 4-quart soup pot, sauté the garlic, onion, and pumpkin in the oil until the onion becomes transparent. Add the apple juice, cover, and bring to a boil. Turn down to simmer until the pumpkin completely breaks down, approximately 25–30 minutes.

While the pumpkin is simmering, toast the fennel, cumin, and coriander seeds on high heat in a dry skillet, stirring constantly, until the seeds are light brown. Grind the seeds with a mortar and pestle or in a small coffee or spice grinder. It is important to grind the spices until they are powder; coriander, especially, can be very crunchy if it is not ground all the way.

Blend the pumpkin mixture in a food processor until smooth. Add the rest of the ingredients and mix well. Put back on low heat but do not boil. Serve immediately.

Note: Sugar pie pumpkins have a lower water content and higher sugar content than traditional pumpkins.

Yield: 4 servings

Lentil-Tomato Harvest Soup

The waning of summer brings on a chill that you feel mid- to late afternoon. Although summer is still in your heart and your bones, by the time the fall sun is past high noon you realize that a little heat is needed to keep your spirits up. This soup is just the ticket.

In a large, covered soup pot on high heat, bring the lentils and water to a boil. Turn down to low and let simmer for 40 minutes.

In a large skillet on high heat, sauté the garlic, onion, and tomato in the oil until the onion becomes transparent. Turn to low heat and add the red wine. Let cook for 5 minutes.

Add the onion and tomato mixture to the lentils. Stir in the thyme, chili powder, cumin, cayenne, corn, bell peppers, honey, and salt. Cook another 20 minutes and serve.

Yield: 6–8 servings

2 cups brown lentils

8 cups water

2 tablespoons minced garlic

2 cups diced onion

3 cups diced fresh tomatoes

4 tablespoons olive oil

½ cup red wine

2 teaspoons dried thyme

2 teaspoons chili powder

2 teaspoons ground cumin

¼ teaspoon cayenne

1 cup corn kernels (fresh, frozen, or drained canned)

1 cup diced green bell peppers

2 tablespoons honey

4 teaspoons salt

Shakow Quince Soup

*I prided myself on being a "fruit lover" until I met Don Shakow. His passion
for growing and eating fruit was as prolific as his fruit trees. He planted his orchard in
our little town of Indianola with over 200 trees and over 100 varieties of fruit on just one acre
of land. And his orchard bears many unusual and exotic fruits one would not expect
to find in the Pacific Northwest, including quince, fig, persimmon, paw-paws, and kiwi.
Although most people think these crops cannot survive successfully in the
Northwest, Don proved otherwise. I now have kiwi and fig in my orchard,
much to my delight, and I celebrate every showing of fruit with wonder.*

*Don introduced me to quince, and this soup is one of my favorite
ways to use it. Quince has an applelike flavor, and when it is cooked, it has
about the same texture. However, it is much harder in body when raw
(use a very sharp knife when cutting it up, and be especially careful!).*

2 tablespoons minced garlic

2 cups diced onion

4 cups cored and minced quince

4 tablespoons butter

5 cups apple juice

1 tablespoon peeled and minced gingerroot

1 cup cream or plain yogurt

Zest of 1 lemon

1 teaspoon garam masala

1 teaspoon curry powder

2 tablespoons sugar

2 teaspoons salt

In a heavy-bottomed 4-quart soup pot, sauté the garlic, onion, and quince in the butter until the onion becomes transparent. Add the apple juice and cover. Bring to a boil and turn down to simmer. Let simmer for 25 minutes, or until the quince becomes soft.

Blend in a food processor until smooth. Put back in the soup pot and return to low heat on the stove. Add the cream or yogurt, lemon zest, garam masala, curry powder, sugar, and salt. Serve immediately.

Yield: 4 servings

Shiitake—Orange Blossom Soup

*Orange-flower water is a lovely item to keep in your pantry. In the
Middle East it is used liberally in many dishes, as is rose water. The experience of
the aroma simultaneously with the light taste of orange blossom is like an aphrodisiac.
At the cafe we use it in many ways. I have added it to carrot or squash soups, made Orange
Blossom Dressing (p. 141) and other dressings with it, and added it to cakes, such as
Orange Blossom Cake (p. 144). Add it in small amounts as you experiment because the
flavor is strong—a few drops go a long way. For the sheer delight of feeling as though
you're in an orange grove while you're braving the Northwest autumn rains, try it!*

Reconstitute the shiitake mushrooms by soaking them in hot water for 20 minutes. Drain, thinly slice, and set aside.

In a medium-sized, heavy-bottomed pot, sauté the garlic and onion in the oil until the onion becomes transparent. Add the shiitakes and meadow mushrooms and sauté for another 2 minutes. Add the water. Bring to a boil. Cover and turn down to simmer for 20 minutes.

Add the orange zest and juice, cream, orange-flower water, salt, and marsala. Let simmer for another 2 minutes. Serve.

Yield: 4–6 servings

4 ounces dried shiitake mushrooms

2 tablespoons minced garlic

4 cups finely diced onion

⅓ cup canola oil

4 cups sliced meadow mushrooms

4 cups water

Zest of 1 orange

¾ cup freshly squeezed orange juice

⅔ cup heavy cream

4 teaspoons orange-flower water

2½ teaspoons salt

3 tablespoons marsala

Pumpkin, White Bean, and Ancho Chile Soup

*Although the ingredients in this soup may sound heavy, much like
the feelings one might have with the first cold days of autumn, the light brothy
flavor with orange carries the lightness of summer days.*

2 tablespoons minced garlic

2 cups diced onion

2 cups peeled and cubed pumpkin

4 tablespoons olive oil

⅔ cup dried cannellini beans, cooked, or 1 (19-ounce) can cannellini beans, drained

4 cups water

1 large or 2 small ancho chiles, soaked, seeded, and chopped (see Note)

1 tablespoon minced fresh rosemary

Zest of 1 orange

½ cup freshly squeezed orange juice

½ cup chopped parsley

1 tablespoon salt

2 tablespoons honey

½ cup freshly grated pecorino Romano cheese

In a large soup pot on high heat, sauté the garlic, onion, and pumpkin in the olive oil until the onion becomes transparent. Add the cannellini beans and water. Cover and bring to a boil. Turn heat to low and cook for another ½ hour.

Add the ancho chiles, rosemary, orange zest and juice, parsley, salt, and honey. Cook another 10 minutes.

Sprinkle Romano cheese on top and serve.

Note: Ancho chiles are the dried version of poblano chiles. They are large compared to jalapeño or serrano chiles. They also vary in heat, so when cooking with them I always like to taste the purée after soaking and taking the seeds out before I continue with a dish. I heat water to just below boiling, when there are little bubbles but not a full rolling boil, add the chiles, turn off the heat, cover them, and soak them for 10 minutes. Then I drain them and, wearing rubber gloves and working under cool running water, make a tear down one side of each chile and pull the seeds out.

Yield: 4–6 servings

Fettuccine with Walnuts, Asiago, and Spinach

This pasta dish combines four of my favorite ingredients to make a very full-flavored meal.

Cook fettuccine al dente.

In a large skillet on medium-high heat, sauté the garlic and onion in the olive oil until the onion becomes transparent. Add the spinach and marsala and cover for 2 minutes to let the spinach wilt. Add the cooked pasta, stirring constantly. Add the Savory Carrot-Thyme Tomato Sauce and toss until the pasta is evenly coated. Add the walnuts, Asiago, basil, lemon zest, and salt. Stir until all ingredients are evenly distributed. Serve immediately.

Note: For a completely different rendition of this dish, omit the Savory Carrot-Thyme Tomato Sauce. Increase the amount of garlic to 6 tablespoons, and be sure to use a really good, fruity olive oil.

Yield: 4 servings

1 pound dry fettuccine

2 tablespoons minced garlic

2 cups diced onion

4 tablespoons olive oil

2 cups spinach leaves, packed

½ cup marsala

3½ cups Savory Carrot-Thyme Tomato Sauce (p. 32)

1 cup lightly toasted walnuts

2 cups grated Asiago cheese

¼ cup chopped fresh basil

1 teaspoon lemon zest

1 teaspoon salt

Four Mushroom Risotto

This dish is made up of ingredients that, for me, define a quintessential Italian tradition. The staple of Arborio rice (especially when it's made with a mushroom stock such as porcini) tossed with seasonal wild mushrooms satisfies my sublime need for food that imports a sense of earthiness in taste and smell.

4 teaspoons minced garlic

1 cup diced onion

4 tablespoons olive oil

4 cups wild mushrooms: chanterelles, morels, oyster mushrooms, and shiitakes, or any other combination

6 cups Basic Risotto (recipe follows)

½ cup marsala

2 cups vegetable or mushroom stock

1 cup fresh chopped parsley

1 cup grated Parmigiano-Reggiano cheese

1 tablespoon minced lemon zest

Salt and pepper to taste

In a medium-sized skillet on medium-high heat, sauté the garlic and onion in the olive oil until the onion becomes transparent. Add the mushrooms and stir for a minute or two, until the mushrooms wilt a bit. Turn heat to medium, add the risotto, and stir in the marsala. After that cooks off, add the vegetable or mushroom stock (you may need a little more, depending on how quickly the liquid evaporates when cooking), and continue to stir to keep the rice from sticking. When the risotto is just about done (soft and chewy, not crunchy, not mushy), stir in the parsley, Parmigiano-Reggiano, lemon zest, and salt and pepper to taste. Serve immediately.

Note: I love to make mushroom stock to "cook off" this risotto by grinding dried porcini, shiitakes, or morels into a powder and steeping the powder in hot water. You can control how strong it is simply by how much mushroom powder you add and for how long you let the stock steep. You can also experiment and decide with which mushroom flavor you prefer to infuse the rice.

Yield: 4–6 servings

Basic Risotto

In a heavy-bottomed 4-quart pot, sauté the garlic and onion in the oil until the onion becomes transparent. Add the arborio rice and salt and brown lightly. Add the 1½ cups of water and the marsala and bring to a boil. Turn down to a simmer and keep stirring, adding 1 cup of water or stock at a time as the rice starts sticking to the pan. Continue adding the water or stock until the rice has absorbed enough liquid to be soft and a little chewy. Stir in the lemon zest and pepper.

Storage: Cooked Basic Risotto will keep in a tightly lidded container in the refrigerator for up to 1 week.

1½ tablespoons minced garlic
1½ cups minced onion
2½ tablespoons olive oil
2 cups arborio rice
1¼ teaspoons salt
¾ cup water
¼ cup marsala
2½ cups water, vegetable stock, or chicken stock
Zest of 1 lemon
¼ teaspoon black pepper

Note: Risotto is fun because you can cook it to just before done, and then finish cooking it off with whatever flavor or theme you want. Although it is a traditional Italian meal, one of my favorite ways to prepare risotto is to give it a Thai twist and finish cooking it off with Coconut-Curry-Lime Sauce (p. 103) and a handful of prawns or rock shrimp, spinach, and snow peas.

For a Mexican theme, finish it off with Anaheim chiles, sweet Roma tomatoes, pepper Jack cheese, thyme, and oregano. Another favorite of mine is a breakfast risotto, prepared like a rice pudding and finished with coconut milk, dates, toasted coconut, toasted almonds, currants, cinnamon, and nutmeg. There is no limit to the versatility of risotto!

Yield: 4–6 servings (6 cups cooked)

CAFE PIZZA

It takes only about 10 minutes (if that) to make this dough, and then you can put any combination of ingredients you like on top. These pizzas can be a quick, elegant snack or a quick, easy meal!

DOUGH:

2 envelopes active dry yeast

3 tablespoons honey

2 cups warm water

3 tablespoons good olive oil

1 teaspoon salt

6 cups unbleached white flour plus additional as needed

In a medium-sized mixing bowl, dissolve the yeast and the honey in the warm water until the yeast begins to bubble. Add the olive oil and salt and, with a whisk or dough hook, add 2 cups of the flour until fully combined. Continue stirring, adding ½ cup of flour at a time until the dough pulls away from the edges of the bowl. Place in a clean, lightly oiled bowl, cover, and let rise until it doubles in size.

Preheat the oven to 450°F. Cut the dough into four equal-sized pieces. Roll into rounds approximately ¼ inch thick. Spread your choice of toppings over the dough, place the pizzas on baking sheets, and bake for 12–15 minutes.

Yield: Four 10-inch pizzas

FAVORITE TOPPINGS:

- Fresh figs, toasted pine nuts, chèvre, caramelized onions, spinach, and a drizzle of good olive oil on top
- Prawns, scallops, feta cheese, basil, garlic, and olive oil
- Caramelized onions, portobello mushrooms, Montrachet, herbs, and a drizzle of good olive oil on top
- Caramelized onions, Comice pears, chèvre, toasted walnuts, and herbs

Steamed Halibut in Spicy Yogurt Sauce

My favorite late-summer or early-fall evening activity is to sit in the garden at the cafe, listening to the tinkling of the fountain in the pond and enjoying the swan song of summer while eating the last of the season's fresh halibut in this cool yogurt sauce. I serve fresh Mango Chutney (p. 138) and rice with it.

In a small, dry skillet on high heat, toast the coriander and cumin seeds, stirring constantly, until they are light brown. Grind to a very fine powder with a mortar and pestle or in a small coffee or spice grinder.

In a medium-sized bowl, whisk together the yogurt, coriander, cumin, garam masala, gingerroot, garlic, lemon zest and juice, cayenne, and sugar.

If you don't have a steamer to cook the fish, put the white wine or vegetable stock in a skillet. Lay the fillets directly in the liquid, cover, and cook on medium-high heat until you see the steam coming out the sides of the lid. Turn to low immediately and cook until the fish just barely flakes apart, approximately 8–10 minutes.

1 teaspoon whole coriander seed

1 teaspoon whole cumin seed

2 cups plain yogurt

1 teaspoon garam masala

1 tablespoon minced fresh gingerroot

1 teaspoon minced garlic

Zest and juice of 2 lemons

$\frac{1}{16}$ teaspoon cayenne

2 tablespoons sugar

2 cups white wine or vegetable stock

4 halibut fillets, about 5 ounces each

Make a pool of the sauce on each of four plates. Place the fillets on top of the sauce and serve immediately.

Storage: The yogurt sauce will keep in a tightly lidded container in the refrigerator for up to 4 days.

Yield: 4 servings

Spicy Ancho Chile and Fresh Mozzarella Tamales

*Tamales are a favorite menu item at the cafe. We make them almost every day,
and fill them with whatever strikes the cook's fancy. Simple, buttery cheese tamales,
pork or prawn tamales, wild blackberry tamales, garden vegetable tamales—whatever they
are filled with, they are delicious. Traditionally tamales are made with lard, but
we make them with butter for a great vegetarian version.*

18 cornhusks

¾ pound (3 sticks) butter

1½ teaspoons salt

1½ teaspoons baking powder

¾ cup milk

¾ cup whole corn kernels

1½ cups masa harina

4 ancho chiles, soaked, seeded, and puréed (see Note, p. 22)

2 cups grated Parmesan cheese

1 pound fresh mozzarella, sliced in ⅛-inch rounds

Two-Squash Salsa (p. 111)

Soak the cornhusks in hot water to soften while you are preparing the dough.

In a medium-sized mixing bowl, beat the butter, salt, and baking powder until light in color and very fluffy. Set aside.

In a food processor, blend the milk and corn into a pulp.

In another medium-sized mixing bowl, stir the milk and corn mixture into the masa until fully incorporated. Add the masa mixture gradually to the butter mixture, beating continuously, until it is fully incorporated. Stir in the ancho chile purée and grated Parmesan.

Using a ¼-cup scoop, divide the dough evenly among 15 of the cornhusks. Flatten the dough and place a piece of fresh mozzarella in each tamale. Wrap the husk around the dough. Tear the other 3 cornhusks into long strips to tie each end of the tamales. In a steamer, cook for 10–12 minutes, covered, until they expand or begin to ooze out of their wrappers a little bit. Serve immediately with Two-Squash Salsa.

Yield: 15 tamales

Halibut Roulades with Spinach and Sun-Dried Tomatoes

For years I have had the honor of receiving gifts of fresh halibut right off the boat from my sister Beth and her husband, Frank. They live in Port Townsend, a beautiful little seaside town near me, and they have a gorgeous wooden tender boat, the Shearwater.

I once heard that the age of a halibut in years can be determined by its weight in pounds. Since halibut can grow to be 400 pounds and more, my understanding is that they can live to be 400 years old. When I learned this, I started feeling a bit more reverent about this fish, even though it already is one of my favorites.

In a large skillet, sauté the onion and garlic in the oil until the onion becomes transparent. Add the spinach leaves and sherry and cook briefly until the leaves wilt. Let cool. In a medium-sized bowl, mix the onion and spinach mixture with the chèvre, herbs, and sun-dried tomatoes.

Slice the halibut fillet in half so that each piece is about 3x6 inches. Place your palm on top of one piece, and, using a very sharp knife, cut on a horizontal plane, slicing crosswise ⅛ inch below your palm. You should get four ⅛-inch-thick slices from each piece that are suitable for rolling.

Put a heaping tablespoon of filling near one end of each halibut slice and roll it up, continuing until all the slices are filled.

Pour the wine or stock into a large skillet. Place the fish roulades gently in the liquid. Cover and turn heat to high. As soon as you see steam coming out the sides of the lid, turn to low. Cook 3–5 more minutes. Serve in a pool of Savory Carrot-Thyme Tomato Sauce.

Yield: 4 servings

1 cup minced onion

1 tablespoon minced garlic

4 tablespoons olive or canola oil

2 cups spinach leaves, packed

2 tablespoons sherry

1 cup chèvre

¼ cup minced fresh green herbs (I like to use a mix of basil, chives, and Greek oregano)

1 cup sun-dried tomatoes, reconstituted and slivered

1 (20-ounce) halibut fillet in one piece (ideally about 3x12 inches in size)

2 cups white wine or vegetable stock

Savory Carrot-Thyme Tomato Sauce (p. 32)

Cranberry-Orange Sauce and Relish

This sauce is lovely with Sweet Potato Blintzes (p. 8) or Sourdough Waffles (p. 122). Like other fruit sauces we make at the cafe, it works just as well with poultry (especially turkey) and seafood. During the holidays I serve smoked trout or duck breast in this sauce.

The relish is the raw version of the sauce and is my favorite condiment with turkey or chicken.

SAUCE:

1 (12-ounce) bag fresh cranberries

½ cup sugar

Zest of 2 oranges

1½ cups freshly squeezed orange juice

¼ cup Triple Sec

RELISH:

1 (12-ounce) bag fresh cranberries

½ cup sugar

Zest of 2 oranges

For the Sauce: In a 2-quart saucepan, bring all of the ingredients to a boil. Turn heat down and simmer until the cranberries break down, approximately 20 minutes.

Sauce Storage: This sauce will keep in a tightly lidded container in the refrigerator for up to 2 weeks.

Yield: About 2½ cups

For the Relish: Blend all ingredients in a food processor until the cranberries are finely chopped.

Relish Storage: This relish will keep in a tightly lidded container in the refrigerator for up to 1 week.

Yield: About 2 cups

SALSAS AND CHUTNEYS

I love to combine opposites to create a balanced, full flavor: sweet and sour, raw and cooked, hot and cold. Salsas and chutneys are a staple in our cafe kitchen to keep that balance. You can make them out of any fruits, vegetables, or legumes. They provide visually flattering, fresh-tasting, and largely nonfat accents to almost any dish, whether it be soup, grain, eggs, beans, fish, or poultry.

When you are making fruit chutney or salsa, you'll find that the fruit will vary in flavor and sugar content according to the degree of ripeness and the season. For the recipes in this book, you can begin with half the indicated amount of sweetener if the fruit is ripe and has a high sugar content, adding ½ to 1 teaspoon at a time after that to taste. If the fruit is not so ripe, usually a bit more sugar (maybe a teaspoon), and more lemon or lime (maybe a tablespoon) will be needed to pull out the fullest flavor of the fruit.

I use salsa and chutney on top of soups, burritos, omelets, and fish, or on the side for dipping and mixing to your taste. Examples of the "opposites attract" idea are Curried Oyster Scramble (p. 6) with Papaya–Red Pepper Salsa (p. 112), Lentil-Tomato Harvest Soup (p. 19) with Two-Squash Salsa (p. 111), and Steamed Halibut in Spicy Yogurt Sauce (p. 27) with Mango Chutney (p. 138).

People always ask me what the difference is between a salsa and a chutney. My understanding is that they illustrate the same idea, carried out in different parts of the world with different spicing. Both are additions that accent the flavors of a dish or a meal. Both use a variety of fruits, vegetables, and legumes. Both use cooked and/or raw ingredients; some type of acid, such as lemon juice, lime juice, or vinegar; often an ingredient with heat, such as ginger or hot peppers; and sometimes a sweetener.

I always keep large amounts of chutneys and salsas around because they are so versatile and extraordinary in their capacity to heighten a meal's attraction. With a good chutney or salsa on top, an ordinary dish becomes an event.

Savory Carrot-Thyme Tomato Sauce

*This is a lovely twist to your basic tomato herb sauce. Instead of cooking
the tomatoes, I blend them in raw to give the sauce a fresh taste. The raw tomatoes also
heighten the color of the carrots so that the sauce is almost Day-Glo orange.*

*I use this with pastas, such as Fettucine with Walnuts, Asiago, and Spinach (p. 23),
or with Halibut Roulades (p. 29). You can be as inventive with it as you might be with a
standard tomato sauce—use it on pizzas, pastas, seafood, or poultry. Enjoy!*

3 tablespoons minced garlic

2 cups minced onion

3 cups cubed carrots

4 tablespoons olive oil

2 teaspoons thyme

3 bay leaves

¾ cup marsala

1 cup water

3 cups chopped Roma tomatoes

4 teaspoons balsamic vinegar

¼ teaspoon cayenne

4 teaspoons salt

1 tablespoon sugar or honey

¼ cup minced fresh oregano

¼ cup minced fresh basil

In a 3-quart saucepan, sauté the garlic, onion, and carrots in the olive oil until the onion becomes transparent. Add the thyme, bay leaves, marsala, and water. Cover and bring to a boil. Turn to low and simmer for 35–40 minutes, until the carrots are completely soft. Blend in a food processor with the raw tomatoes, in two batches, until the sauce is completely smooth and bright orange. Put back in the pot and return to the stove on low heat. Add the balsamic vinegar, cayenne, salt, sugar or honey, oregano, and basil.

Storage: This sauce will keep in a tightly lidded container in the refrigerator for up to 1 week.

Yield: 4–6 servings

Ancho Chile—Tamarind Sauce

This sauce has a bit of smoky darkness that reminds me of fall and the coming of longer nights. It can be used like a dipping sauce for chips, or in the same way that you might use sour cream—although it's rather spicy, so a little bit goes a long way. You can use it on top of eggs, chicken, pork, or rice, or as an addition to many other sauces to enrich their flavor.

In a food processor or a blender, process the ancho chiles, lime zest and juice, garlic, and tamarind paste for approximately 2 minutes, or until the purée is smooth. Pour into a large mixing bowl and stir in the sour cream, cilantro, sugar, and salt.

Storage: This sauce will keep in a tightly lidded container in the refrigerator for up to 1 week.

Yield: 5½ cups

10 ancho chiles, about 6 ounces, soaked and seeded (see Note, p. 22)

Zest and juice of 5 limes

2 tablespoons minced garlic

¼ cup tamarind paste

4 cups sour cream

1 cup cilantro leaves, packed

¼ cup sugar

2 tablespoons salt

Roasted Tomatillo—Green Pepper Sauce

*This sauce has repeatedly shown up on our brunch menu since we
opened the cafe. Every time I offer it, someone comes up to me and says, "I can
never figure out how to use tomatillos—can I have this recipe?" As with many sauces that
titillate the senses, one finds oneself drawn to "that last bite," cleaning the plate with a crust of
bread. I have used this sauce on top of burritos, under grilled fish, over eggs, and, believe
it or not, tossed with noodles. Decide what the foundation of your dish will be, and
if this sauce sounds like an accent in the right direction—go with it!*

4 cups (about 2 pounds) tomatillos, husked and sliced in half

2 green bell peppers, seeded and cut in quarters lengthwise

1 jalapeño pepper, cut in half lengthwise and seeded

½ cup whole peeled garlic cloves

2 large sweet yellow onions, peeled and cut in quarters vertically

½ cup olive oil

1 cup sour cream

1 tablespoon fresh oregano

Zest and juice of 1 lime

½ cup fresh cilantro leaves

2 teaspoons ground cumin

1 tablespoon sugar

2 teaspoons salt

Preheat oven to 450°F.

On a large rimmed baking sheet, lay the tomatillos, flat side down, the green peppers, jalapeño pepper, garlic cloves, and onions. Drizzle the olive oil over the vegetables and roast in the oven for 45 minutes or until the tops of the tomatillos and onions are dark brown.

In a food processor or blender, blend all of the roasted vegetables until they are a smooth purée. Put into a large mixing bowl.

Add the sour cream, oregano, lime zest and juice, cilantro, cumin, sugar, and salt. Whisk all together to make a smooth, creamy sauce. Keep refrigerated.

Storage: This sauce will keep in a tightly lidded container in the refrigerator for up to 1 week.

Yield: About 6 cups

AUTUMN CORDIALS

At my family's last reunion we all gathered, bringing along various ingredients to cook with or intoxicating spirits with which to welcome in the evening's song and conversation. Two of my sisters, Beth and Jan, brought cordials made from berries freshly gathered in season—Beth had made a blackberry cordial and Jan a strawberry cordial. Sitting in the back garden, soaking in the afternoon sun, luxuriating in the slow, relaxed conversation that derives from years of growing up together, we sipped our cordials and simultaneously tasted the sweetness of the moment. This is their recipe.

4 cups blackberries or strawberries, mashed

4 cups vodka

1 cinnamon stick (for the blackberry cordial)

Dash of almond extract (for the strawberry cordial)

2 cups sugar, or less, to taste

Combine the mashed berries, vodka, and cinnamon stick or almond extract in a tightly lidded container and let sit for up to 1 month. Strain through a sieve lined with cheesecloth and discard berries. Add the sugar to the liquid and stir until dissolved. Bottle and store in a cool, dark place. It will keep indefinitely, although with some loss of color over time. Serve over ice, or with a dash of seltzer, or over ice cream.

Yield: 1 quart

Chocolate Mousse Cake

This cake never ceases to turn heads when we walk through the cafe with it.
No less impressive is the flavor.

6 ounces bittersweet chocolate

6 tablespoons unsweetened cocoa

6 tablespoons water

½ pound (2 sticks) butter, at room temperature

1 cup brown sugar

6 eggs, separated

1 teaspoon vanilla

¼ cup sour cream

½ teaspoon salt

2 cups cake flour, sifted before measuring

2 teaspoons baking soda

2 teaspoons boiling water

⅛ teaspoon cream of tartar

½ cup white sugar

1 cup hazelnuts

1 recipe Vanilla Buttercream (recipe follows)

2–3 tablespoons Frangelico (optional)

1 recipe Chocolate Mousse (p. 114)

1 recipe Chocolate Cream Glaze (recipe follows)

Grease and flour three 9-inch round cake pans. Preheat oven to 375°F.

In a small, heavy saucepan on low heat, melt the chocolate and set aside to cool.

In another small, heavy saucepan on low heat, whisk the cocoa and water until the mixture thickens and leaves a bare trail when the whisk is drawn across the bottom of the pan. Set aside to cool.

With an electric mixer, whip the butter on high speed until it becomes light in color and doubles in size, approximately 5 minutes. Continuing whipping while adding the brown sugar, 1 tablespoon at a time, until all of the sugar is incorporated. Whip on high speed for 5 more minutes. Add the egg yolks, one at a time, whipping well after each addition.

Add the cooled cocoa mixture, the cooled chocolate mixture, and the vanilla, in that order, whipping well after each addition.

With the mixer on medium speed, add the sour cream and whip until it is fully incorporated. Pour into a large mixing bowl and set aside.

In a small mixing bowl, add the salt to the sifted cake flour. Set aside.

Place the baking soda in a small stainless steel bowl. Add the boiling water. The mixture should fizz.

Sift one third of the flour/salt mixture over the chocolate batter, add the water/soda mixture, and fold in. Add another third of the flour, folding it gently into the batter until it is all folded, and then the last third. Fold it in gently, but do not overmix.

Whip the egg whites until they become frothy. Continuing to whip, add the cream of tartar and then the white sugar, 1 tablespoon at a time. Whip until the whites form stiff peaks. Gently fold them into the cake batter.

Divide the batter evenly among the three cake pans. Bake at 375°F for 5 minutes, then turn down to 350°F and bake for 10–15 minutes more, or until the cake springs back when you lightly touch it. Let layers cool in the pans for 5 minutes, and then invert onto cooling racks.

On a baking sheet, toast the hazelnuts in the oven at 350°F for 10–15 minutes. Roll in a towel to peel off the skins. Grind in a food processor and set aside.

Prepare the Vanilla Buttercream, adding the ground hazelnuts. If you are feeling decadent, add 2–3 tablespoons of Frangelico.

Prepare the Chocolate Mousse.

Prepare the Chocolate Cream Glaze.

To assemble the cake: Place one layer of the chocolate cake in a 9-inch springform pan. Spread a thin layer of the buttercream on the cake and top it with half of the chocolate mousse. Place the second layer of cake on top and repeat the process. Place the final layer of cake on top, ice it with buttercream, and pour the chocolate glaze over the top. Cover and refrigerate overnight.

Yield: One 9-inch three-layered cake

Vanilla Buttercream

Vanilla buttercream can be used as the sole icing for a cake, or as a filling in thin layers with fresh fruit or chocolate mousse. You can also add lemon or orange zest to it.

¾ pound (3 sticks) unsalted butter, at room temperature

5 egg whites

1 cup and 2 tablespoons sugar

Pinch of salt

¼ teaspoon vanilla

In a medium-sized mixing bowl with an electric mixer, whip the butter on high speed for approximately 10 minutes, or until the butter turns a light color and almost doubles in size. Set aside.

In a double boiler, whisk the egg whites and sugar for 3–5 minutes, until the sugar dissolves. Pour the mixture into a large bowl. With the electric mixer on high, whip the egg whites and sugar until they form stiff, glossy peaks. Turn the mixer to low speed, and add the whipped butter 2 tablespoons at a time. When all of the butter is incorporated, turn mixer to high speed again and whip for 3–5 minutes. If the buttercream separates, don't worry. Whip a little longer and it will cream up again.

Note: This buttercream is best used the day it is made. However, it can be frozen and re-whipped after being brought back to room temperature.

Yield: Enough to fill and frost one 9-inch three-layered cake

Chocolate Cream Glaze

"Why eat anything else?" (a quote from a customer)

Chop both kinds of chocolate into small pieces and put them into a small stainless steel bowl. Heat the cream just to the boiling point, pour over the chocolate, and cover. Let sit for 5 minutes, then uncover and stir until the glaze is smooth and creamy. Use immediately.

Note: For chocolate rum glaze, substitute 2 tablespoons dark rum for 2 tablespoons of the heavy cream.

Yield: Enough to glaze one 9-inch cake

4 ounces semisweet chocolate

1 ounce unsweetened chocolate

½ cup and 2 tablespoons heavy cream

Hazelnut Torte with Chocolate Rum Buttercream

My family moved to Vashon Island when I was 14. To my surprise, there were large orchards of nut trees—walnut, hazelnut, and almond—even in our backyard, growing to a ripe old age in the Northwest climate. Until that point I had no idea that nuts grew in the Northwest. I worked for a season at Wax Orchards on Vashon Island, where they grow both fruits and nuts as well as make jams, jellies, and other products. Since that time, I now recognize many nut trees with some age etched into their trunks around the Puget Sound region.

This torte is an elegant, not-too-sweet dessert.

---

1 recipe Chocolate Rum Buttercream (recipe follows)

1 cup chocolate rum glaze (see Note, p. 39)

TORTE:

2 cups hazelnuts

6 eggs, separated

9 tablespoons plus 9 tablespoons sugar

⅛ teaspoon salt

⅛ teaspoon cream of tartar

6 tablespoons cake flour, sifted before measuring (see Note, below)

2 tablespoons rum

Prepare the Chocolate Rum Buttercream and the chocolate rum glaze.

Preheat oven to 350°F.

Grease three 8-inch round cake pans and dust with flour or line with parchment.

On a baking sheet, toast the hazelnuts in the oven for 10–15 minutes. Roll in a towel to peel off the skins. Grind in a food processor and set aside. Raise oven heat to 375°.

With an electric mixer, whip the egg yolks on high speed until they triple in volume, approximately 5 minutes. Continue whipping on medium speed while adding 9 tablespoons of the sugar, 1 tablespoon at a time. Turn to high speed and whip for 3–5 more minutes. Pour into a large mixing bowl and set aside.

With an electric mixer on medium speed, whip the egg whites for 1 minute. Continue whipping and add the salt and the cream of tartar. Add the other 9 tablespoons of sugar, 1 tablespoon at a time, continuing to whip the egg whites until they form stiff peaks. Set aside.

Sift the cake flour over the yolk mixture and gently fold it in. Add the rum in a thin stream and fold it in. Sprinkle the ground hazelnuts over the batter and fold in.

Add the whipped egg whites in three parts, folding in gently each time.

Divide the batter equally among the three cake pans. Bake at 375°F for 5 minutes. Turn down to 350°F and bake for 10–15 minutes more. Let cool in pans for 5 minutes and then invert the layers onto cooling racks.

To assemble the torte: Place one layer of the cake on a cake plate. Spread a thin layer of the buttercream over the top. Place the second layer on top of the bottom layer and repeat the process, ending with the top layer of the cake. Ice the top and sides of the torte with the buttercream, and let it chill in the refrigerator for 15 minutes. Take the torte out of the refrigerator and spread the chocolate glaze over the top, allowing excess to drizzle down the sides of the torte. Chill for ½ hour to set.

You can make the torte the day before and take out of the refrigerator 1 hour before serving to bring to room temperature. The unfinished torte freezes very well for up to 2 weeks.

Note: For those who are allergic to wheat, you can substitute cornstarch for the flour. We did this for the bride when we catered a wedding recently.

Yield: One 8-inch three-layered torte

Chocolate Rum Buttercream

*We use this for the preceding Hazelnut Torte. I try to keep bowls
of extra buttercream around for those "spur of the moment" orders for
chocolate cake or white cake with a chocolate buttercream filling.*

4 ounces bittersweet chocolate

4 tablespoons water

4 tablespoons unsweetened cocoa

6 tablespoons (¾ stick) unsalted butter, at room temperature

¾ cup brown sugar

2 egg yolks

1 whole egg

½ teaspoon vanilla

2 tablespoons dark rum

Melt the chocolate on low heat in a double boiler and let cool.

In a heavy-bottomed saucepan, whisk together the water and cocoa on low heat until the mixture thickens. It is thick enough when you run the whisk through it and the whisk leaves a bare trail on the bottom of the pan. Set aside to cool.

With an electric mixer, whip the butter on high speed until it is light-colored and doubled in size. Add the brown sugar, 1 tablespoon at a time, while continuing to whip on high speed, until all of the brown sugar is incorporated. Whip 5 more minutes.

Turn the mixer to medium speed and add the egg yolks. While whipping, add the whole egg, then the vanilla, and then the rum. Continue whipping for 1 more minute after all of these ingredients are incorporated. Turn mixer to high, add the cooled chocolate and the cocoa mixture, and whip on high for 3 minutes longer.

Note: This buttercream is best used just as soon as it is made and does not store as well as standard buttercream.

Yield: Enough to fill and frost one 8-inch three-layered torte

WINTER

Warming Winter Fare

BREAKFAST:
Holiday Scramble with Persimmon and Spinach

LUNCH:
Mexican Fish Cakes with Avocado—Pumpkin Seed Salsa

DINNER:
Roasted Apple and Ginger Bisque, Seared Pork Tenderloin with
Spicy Green Apple—Tequila Sauce, Basic Polenta

WiNTEr

———

THE PUGET SOUND COUNTRY could lay claim to the famous Samuel Clemens quote, "The nicest winter I ever spent was a summer in San Francisco." Seattle is famous for fog, rain, gray skies, water, and hills; and, like its southern neighbor, it demands a certain hardiness of character. Spending winter in the Pacific Northwest is a study in survival—not unlike that of the common blackberry vine, which can be cut to the ground and even dug up, yet, miraculously, will produce blackberries in that very spot next season. Spring and summer days make us feel as though we live in paradise: an azure sky reflects the waters that finger their way through every length of land, the sun's warmth bounces off the expanse of surrounding mountain ranges, and lush gardens are full of edible ecstasy. At such times, we tell ourselves, "We *can* put up with winter."

Some people, even locals, however, don't think so. Hawaii, Baja, New Mexico—anywhere south is the preferred destination to wait out the dark months. But I love the rain. Like the Eskimo's 50-odd words for snow, we need as many terms to describe Northwest rains in all their variations, from subtle mist to pelting fury. For me, rain is tactile in the softness of clouds and the smooth slatelike appearance of Puget Sound. Coming inside after a long wet run in the rain is as delicious as the taste of fresh air. Cooking feels good. Fire, warmth, steamy windows, hot tea—even doing the dishes is a welcome activity. Cooking commands use of all our senses and, as a result, it comforts us on all levels.

An old Kalamazoo woodstove stands at the center of the cafe dining room. It is the only source of heat besides the large double oven where we do all our baking. New waitstaff, whether or not they have a history of building successful fires, soon learn this basic skill. For a while our regular customer Peter, whose wife Sydney traveled a lot for her work and whose three children had flown the nest, took on the responsibility of a good hot fire at the cafe, arriving each morning with an armload of dry kindling. When Peter and Sydney moved away, another daily customer—coincidentally named Pete—started stocking the woodpile with boxes of neatly chopped dry kindling for the same purpose. Needless to say, he has also been given a list of odd jobs that will ensure his continued presence at the cafe for a long time to come. His dog Bear awaits the "sausage-toss" through the kitchen window every morning from our canine-loving cook Stephanie. What would we do without our customers?

At this time of the year, I cook with an emphasis on the importance of feeling warm and full, in contrast to summer's focus on feeling light. I wake up to a chilly morning thinking about polenta, beans, burdock root, potatoes, carrots, beets, stews, hearty soups, stuffed breads, and baked squash. Stuffed fish, roulades of all kinds, roasted vegetables, and more all pour into my mind at once, and I'm forced to choose just a few for the day's menu.

In winter, locals fill the cafe, where it's easy to stay warm on all sides: good conversation, discussion of a book someone has recently read, the excited focus of another's latest love, and enduring friendships are all a part of our kitchen and more easily explored during these slower days. Although it may be hard for some of us to walk with pleasure under the gray winter skies of the Pacific Northwest day after day, it's never hard to open the door to the full ovens and steamy soups that make up our winter cafe life.

Green Apple and White Cheddar Omelet

This is an age-old combination that I never tire of. Crisp apples and cheese for lunch, melted Cheddar on apple pie for dessert. Why not an apple-Cheddar omelet for breakfast?

In a small skillet on high heat, sauté the onion in 1 teaspoon of the butter or oil until it softens a bit (about 1 minute). Add the apple, nutmeg, cinnamon, lemon zest, wine, brown sugar, and salt. Stir and set aside.

In a large omelet pan on medium-high heat, melt the other teaspoon of butter or oil. Pour the beaten eggs into the pan, tilting so that they cover the bottom. When the eggs set up, flip the omelet and turn the heat off. Place the cheese on one half of the omelet, spread the apple mixture on top of the cheese, and fold the other half of the omelet over the filling. Let the cheese melt for a minute. Serve with a dollop of sour cream on top.

Yield: 1 serving

¼ cup finely diced onion

2 teaspoons butter or canola oil

¾ cup peeled, cored, and diced green apple (we use Granny Smiths)

Pinch of nutmeg

Pinch of cinnamon

½ teaspoon minced lemon zest

1 tablespoon white wine

1 teaspoon brown sugar

Pinch of salt

3 large eggs, beaten

½ cup grated sharp white Cheddar cheese

Sour cream for topping

Holiday Scramble with Persimmon and Spinach

Persimmons enter the market for just a short few weeks around Christmas, so
I use them in many dishes for breakfast, lunch, and dinner to get my fill of them.
The colors in this scramble—the bright orange-red of the persimmon and the
green of the spinach—are particularly appropriate for Christmas.

¼ cup minced onion

1½ teaspoons butter or canola oil

¼ cup peeled and cubed persimmon

¼ cup peeled, cored, and cubed crisp apple (Granny Smith or Fuji)

½ cup roughly chopped spinach leaves

2 tablespoons late harvest riesling

3 large eggs, beaten

¼ cup grated Gruyère cheese

Pinch of salt

In a medium-sized omelet pan on medium-high heat, sauté the onion in the butter or oil until it becomes transparent. Add the persimmon and apple and stir. Add the spinach and wine, turn down to low, and cover to let the spinach wilt. Uncover and add the eggs, Gruyère, and salt, stirring until the egg is cooked through and the cheese melted.

Yield: 1 serving

Banana-Oatmeal Cakes with Hazelnut Butter

*When I threw these together, I was in a hurry to come up with something
quick for weekend brunch. I was making a pot of oatmeal, thinking about how
uninspired I had been feeling lately. As I watched the bananas blend in with the
morning mush, I realized that, although I love oats, I never make anything with them
for brunch, except oatmeal. Why not something like a johnnycake, I thought, only lighter?
We put these together and cooked one up. Jeannie, our baker, said, "You've got to write
that one down." These make a light, fluffy, melt-in-your-mouth breakfast or brunch.*

For the hazelnut butter: Preheat oven to 350°F. On a baking sheet, toast the hazelnuts in the oven for 10–15 minutes. Roll in a towel to peel off the skins. Grind in a food processor.

Beat the butter until it almost doubles in size and turns light in color. Fold in the ground hazelnuts.

For the banana-oatmeal cakes: In a medium-sized bowl, combine the oats, flour, baking soda, baking powder, salt, sugar, and cardamom. Separate the eggs and beat the whites until they form stiff peaks. Set aside. In another medium-sized bowl, whisk the egg yolks. Add the buttermilk and melted butter and whisk in thoroughly.

With a large spoon, stir the wet ingredients into the dry ingredients. Avoid overmixing. Fold in the sliced banana and the beaten egg whites.

On medium heat, pour the batter into a lightly greased small skillet to make 3½-inch cakes. When small bubbles form on the top of the cakes, flip them. Cook another 3 minutes, or until the cakes spring back when you touch them. Serve them with hazelnut butter and maple syrup.

Yield: 4 servings (8 good-sized cakes)

HAZELNUT BUTTER:
¼ cup hazelnuts
¼ pound (1 stick) butter, at room temperature

BANANA-OATMEAL CAKES:
1 cup rolled oats
1 cup unbleached white flour
2 teaspoons baking soda
1 teaspoon baking powder
½ teaspoon salt
2 tablespoons sugar
½ teaspoon ground cardamom
3 eggs
1 cup buttermilk
6 tablespoons butter, melted
2 teaspoons peeled and grated fresh gingerroot
1 large banana, sliced

Fresh Fig and Montrachet Omelet with Fig Purée

My first experience of fresh figs was in Chico, California, where the fig trees were laden to the ground with the weight of the fruit. The intense heat of Chico and the sweet stickiness of the figs languidly lolled me into sleepiness, and there I slept until I awoke with a bit of a bellyache. Needless to say, I was surprised to find out from my friend Don Shakow, who had a few different kinds of fig trees in his yard, that they grow quite happily in the maritime Northwest. I now have three fig trees in my own yard!

3 cups cubed fresh figs

8 teaspoons butter or canola oil

¼ cup port

1 teaspoon minced lemon zest

4 teaspoons fresh lemon juice

½ teaspoon cinnamon

Pinch of salt

12 large eggs, beaten

8 tablespoons Montrachet cheese

1 cup Fig Purée (recipe follows)

In a small skillet on medium heat, sauté the figs in 4 teaspoons of the butter or oil until they are just heated through. Add the port, lemon zest, lemon juice, cinnamon, and salt to taste. Stir for 1 more minute. Turn off heat and set aside.

Melt a teaspoon of butter in an omelet pan on medium heat. Pour three of the eggs into the pan, being sure they cover the bottom. When the eggs have set up, turn the heat off and flip the omelet. Place 2 tablespoons of the Montrachet cheese on one half of the omelet and cover it with one quarter of the fig mixture. Fold the other half of the omelet over the filling. Let sit for about a minute, or until the cheese warms through. Repeat the process for each omelet.

Pour ¼ cup Fig Purée on top of each omelet and serve.

Yield: 4 servings

Fig Purée

I use this sauce on top of Fresh Fig and Montrachet Omelet (preceding page).
If you are a lover of duck, serve it with this purée for a marriage made in heaven.

Blend all of the ingredients in a food processor until smooth.

Storage: This sauce will keep in a tightly lidded container in the refrigerator for up to 2 weeks.

Yield: About 2½ cups

4 cups fresh figs
½ cup sugar
⅓ cup port
Zest and juice of 3 oranges
2 teaspoons cinnamon
1 teaspoon cardamom
1 teaspoon peeled and minced fresh gingerroot

Buckwheat Cinnamon Waffles with Pear-Ginger Sauce

*Although I often think of buckwheat as heavy, these waffles are
fairly light in texture and full in flavor.*

3 large eggs, separated
⅔ cup buckwheat flour
1⅓ cups unbleached white flour
2 teaspoons baking powder
1 teaspoon baking soda
½ teaspoon salt
1½ cups buttermilk
4 tablespoons butter, melted
Pear-Ginger Sauce (recipe follows)
Cinnamon Cream (p. 11)

Heat the waffle iron.

Beat the egg whites until they form stiff peaks. Set
aside.

Sift all of the dry ingredients together into a
medium-sized mixing bowl. Set aside.

In another medium-sized mixing bowl, whisk the
egg yolks. Continue whisking while adding the
buttermilk and melted butter. Whisk the dry ingredients into the wet ingredients. Avoid overmixing.

Fold the egg whites into the waffle batter.

Grease the waffle iron. Pour ¾ cup batter for each
waffle onto the waffle iron and cook for about
3 minutes.

Serve with Pear-Ginger Sauce. And if you're
feeling particularly decadent, top the sauce with
Cinnamon Cream.

Yield: Five 7-inch waffles

Pear-Ginger Sauce

*I have quite a few different pear trees in my yard, but my favorite
pear is the Comice, purely for its unique flavor. For sauces, however, the softer,
juicier pears, such as Anjou or Bartlett, cook down better.*

*Because I use fruit sauces with main dishes as well as with desserts,
I often make them in large batches to use at my whim. I have used this one
with pork, with chicken, on top of waffles, and over omelets.*

In a medium-sized, heavy-bottomed saucepan on medium heat, cook the pears, apple juice, and muscat canelli until the pears begin to fall apart. Purée in a blender or food processor until smooth. Return to the saucepan on low heat. Add the lemon zest, gingerroot, and sugar or honey. Cook another 5–10 minutes.

Storage: This sauce will keep in a tightly lidded container in the refrigerator for 7–10 days.

Note: For a delicious and more subtly flavored pear purée, you can omit the gingerroot.

Yield: About 5½ cups

6 cups cored and cubed Anjou or Bartlett pears

1 cup apple juice

½ cup muscat canelli

Zest of one lemon, minced

2 tablespoons peeled and minced fresh gingerroot

¼ cup sugar or honey

Mexican Fish Cakes with Avocado—Pumpkin Seed Salsa

*I am not sure which I like better, these fish cakes or this salsa, but make sure
you have plenty of both on hand—you won't be able to stop eating them! These serve
well for breakfast, lunch, or dinner (I guess dessert might be pushing it too far).
They are also delicious with Pineapple-Lime Salsa (p. 139).*

2 pounds fresh halibut fillet

2 tablespoons olive oil

1 minced garlic clove

Salt and pepper

1½ cups minced onion

2 eggs, beaten

1 cup cilantro leaves

1 tablespoon minced garlic

½ cup mayonnaise

½ teaspoon red pepper flakes, or
½ teaspoon minced fresh jalapeño

1½ teaspoons ground cumin

1½ teaspoons chili powder

2 tablespoons minced fresh
oregano

1 tablespoon minced fresh
marjoram

1½ teaspoons salt

1 cup dry bread crumbs

Zest of 1 lemon

Avocado—Pumpkin Seed Salsa
(recipe follows)

Preheat the oven to 350°F.

Rub the halibut fillet down with olive oil, garlic, salt, and pepper. Wrap it in foil and bake it for 15–20 minutes, just until it will flake apart.

Flake the fish into a large mixing bowl. Add the rest of the ingredients and mix thoroughly. Form into 8 equal-sized cakes. Lightly oil a skillet on medium-high heat, and fry the cakes until the edges start turning golden brown. Flip. Fry for another 2–3 minutes. Serve immediately.

Serve with Avocado—Pumpkin Seed Salsa.

Note: You can make up the fish cake mixture a day ahead, refrigerate it, and make it into cakes just before frying.

Yield: 4 servings (8 cakes)

Avocado Pumpkin Seed Salsa

Our "even-keeled, nothing can shake her" night cook, Anne, came up with this idea at one of our tasting dinners when we were testing recipes for this book. Although we use it as a salsa, it is almost like a guacamole in texture, so you could use it as a specialty guacamole as well.

Stir together all ingredients. This salsa is best used immediately.

Yield: 2½ cups

1 cup diced avocado

⅔ cup toasted whole pumpkin seeds

½ cup minced red bell pepper

½ cup sliced black olives

½ cup diced Roma tomatoes

½ cup minced green onion

1 tablespoon minced garlic

Zest and juice of 2 limes

1 teaspoon minced jalapeño

½ cup chopped cilantro leaves

1½ teaspoons salt

2 tablespoons sugar

Sweet Corn and Pepper Muffins

*In the chilly winter months I like to make savory baked goods such as
these muffins. I serve them with scrambled eggs tossed with sharp Cheddar cheese
and spring onion for breakfast, or with chili or a hearty stew for lunch.*

2⅓ cups unbleached white flour

1 cup yellow cornmeal

1 tablespoon baking powder

2 teaspoons baking soda

½ cup granulated sugar

1½ teaspoons salt

4 eggs

1½ cups buttermilk

10 tablespoons butter, melted

2 cups sweet corn (fresh or frozen)

2 cups diced red and green bell peppers

1 cup minced chives

1 cup grated sharp white Cheddar cheese

Preheat oven to 350°F.

In a medium-sized mixing bowl, sift together the flour, cornmeal, baking powder, baking soda, sugar, and salt.

In another medium-sized mixing bowl, whisk the eggs. Whisk in the buttermilk, melted butter, corn, peppers, chives, and cheese. Pour the wet ingredients into the dry ingredients. Stir. Be careful not to overmix.

Spoon into greased muffin tins and bake for 20–25 minutes, until the tops of the muffins spring back when touched.

Yield: 18 medium-sized muffins

Roasted Apple and Ginger Bisque

*My mother's birthday is in mid-November. When she turned 60, we
planned a family gathering at the cafe on Thanksgiving—a time when most
of the family would have a long weekend off for traveling, gathering, and celebrating.
I wanted to make something festive that matched the season as well as the
richness of the occasion. In this bisque, the smoky apple flavor balances
the fresh heat of the ginger nicely without being overwhelming.*

Preheat oven to 450°F.

Toss the apples with the oil and lay them, skin side up, on an 11 x 17-inch baking sheet. Roast in the oven for 40–45 minutes, until the skins are almost black. Let cool and pull skins off. (They should come off easily.)

In a food processor or blender, purée the apples until they are smooth in texture. Set aside.

In a medium-sized, heavy-bottomed pan, sauté the garlic and onion in the butter or oil until the onion becomes transparent. Add the puréed apple, water, apple juice, and gingerroot. Cover and bring to a boil. Turn down to simmer for 20–25 minutes. Add the lemon zest, lemon juice, cardamom, white wine, cream, sugar, and salt. Do not boil. Serve immediately.

Note: To add a touch of celebratory elegance, mix 1 cup of good yogurt with ⅓ cup toasted hazelnuts. Garnish the soup with this. It is delicious!

Yield: 4–6 servings

---

4 pounds Granny Smith apples, quartered and cored

2 tablespoons canola oil

2 tablespoons minced garlic

2 cups diced onion

6 tablespoons butter or canola oil

1 cup water

2½ cups apple juice

2 tablespoons peeled and minced fresh gingerroot

Zest of 1 lemon

⅓ cup freshly squeezed lemon juice

¼ teaspoon ground cardamom

½ cup dry white wine

1½ cups heavy cream (or one of the equivalents given on p. xxi)

1 tablespoon sugar

2½ teaspoons salt

Split Soup of Beet-Lemon and Butternut-Orange

Split soups are one of my favorite dishes to make. They are always beautiful because you are pouring two different soups, with complementary flavors and colors, into the same bowl. This is the most dramatic of split soups because the purple/pink of the beets and the bright orange of the squash command everyone's attention. We in the kitchen usually hear a gasp or two when the waitstaff delivers this soup to a table. Greg and Angela Sutherland, two loyal customers who live near the cafe, had this soup for their wedding meal, followed by a salmon and halibut braid (p. 130) in Lemony Sorrel and Spinach Sauce (p. 109) and sushi—definitely the most elegant, delicious, and beautiful looking meal I have prepared for a wedding to date!

People always ask about the serving technique for split soups. There are three rules to follow. The soups have to be puréed. They have to be of the same thickness and texture so that they will not bleed into each other. The third rule is that you have to pour the two soups into the bowl simultaneously and at the same rate, one with your left hand and the other with your right hand, to make a perfect visual line down the middle.

BEET-LEMON SOUP:

1 tablespoon minced garlic
2 cups diced onion
2½ cups cubed beets
4 tablespoons butter or canola oil
1 cup chopped carrots
2 cups water
Zest of 2 lemons
1½ cups heavy cream (or one of the equivalents given on p. xxi)
1 teaspoon finely chopped fresh dill
2 teaspoons salt
1 tablespoon sugar or honey

For the beet-lemon soup: In a medium-sized soup pot, sauté the garlic, onion, and beets in the butter or oil until the onion becomes transparent. Add the carrots and sauté 1 more minute. Add the water, cover and bring to a boil, and turn down to low heat for ½ hour.

Purée the soup in a blender or food processor until smooth and return to the pot. Add the lemon zest, cream or equivalent, dill, salt, and sugar or honey. Do not boil.

For the butternut-orange soup: In a medium-sized soup pot, sauté the garlic, onion, and squash in the butter or oil until the onion becomes transparent. Add the water, cover and bring to a boil, and turn down to low heat for ½ hour.

Purée the soup in a blender or food processor until smooth and return to the pot. Add the orange zest, cream or equivalent, salt, and sugar or honey. Do not boil.

Combine the two soups in each bowl, following the pouring directions above, and serve immediately.

Yield: 4—6 servings

BUTTERNUT-ORANGE SOUP:

1 tablespoon minced garlic

2 cups diced onion

3½ cups peeled and cubed butternut squash

4 tablespoons butter or canola oil

2 cups water

Zest of 1½ oranges

1½ cups heavy cream (or one of the equivalents given on p. xxi)

2 teaspoons salt

1 tablespoon sugar or honey

SOUPS

A bowl of good soup means comfort: it can soothe, heal, and satisfy the soul.

At the cafe we make soup daily. We make soups out of almost anything—any fruit, vegetable, meat (although we try to stay vegetarian because so many of our customers count on it), grain, legume, or dairy product. We usually spend a great deal of energy coming up with just the right garnish for a soup. We like to marry extremes, in the garnish and the soup—hot and cold, spicy and sweet, fruit and legumes, cooked and raw. The result, consistently, is that many people come in and say, "Whatever the soup is, I'll take it."

The challenge of coming up with a new soup every day, month after month and year after year, is considerable. We do repeat soups, but the fun of stretching and creating is indicative of the spirit of the cafe kitchen. We make puréed soups, chunky soups, brothy and thick soups.

In general, any soup recipe or idea can be a jumping-off point for a finished product. Don't hesitate to follow your instincts with crazy ideas that come into your head! When I first suggested pineapple salsa on top of a bean soup, one of my coworkers looked askance—it did sound strange, but we ate three bowls each. The more you take a leap of faith, even when something sounds really crazy, the more your instincts will be supported by experience and sound knowledge. Have fun!

Black Bean, Lime, and Chile Soup

*This is delicious with sour cream and cilantro or chives on top. For a different accent,
I sometimes toast coriander seed, grind it, and add it to yogurt to put on top.*

¼ cup minced garlic

2½ cups diced onion

1½ cups diced green and red bell peppers

1½ cups diced Anaheim chiles

¼ pound (1 stick) butter, or ½ cup canola oil

3 cups cooked black beans

1½ cups water

3 bay leaves

Zest of 2 limes

¼ cup freshly squeezed lime juice

1½ teaspoons chili powder

⅛ teaspoon cayenne

1 teaspoon ground cumin

¾ teaspoon thyme

¾ teaspoon oregano

1¼ cups roughly chopped cilantro leaves

2 tablespoons sugar

2 teaspoons salt

In a heavy-bottomed 4-quart soup pot, sauté the garlic, onion, green and red bell peppers, and Anaheim chiles in the butter or oil until the onion becomes transparent. Add the black beans, water, and bay leaves. Cover and bring to a boil. Turn down to simmer for ½ hour. Add the lime zest, lime juice, chili powder, cayenne, cumin, thyme, oregano, cilantro, sugar, and salt. Serve immediately.

Yield: 4–6 servings

Curried Lentil Soup with Mango Yogurt

High-quality plain yogurt with chopped fresh fruit stirred into it
adds texture and flavor to many curried soups. You can make this one more
elaborate by adding cilantro or grated fresh gingerroot as well.

In a large soup pot on medium-high heat, sauté the onion, garlic, and lentils in the oil until the onion becomes transparent. Add the water and bay leaves, cover, and bring to a boil. Turn down to low heat and simmer for 40 minutes.

Add the coconut milk, garam masala, gingerroot, lime zest and juice, salt, and sugar or honey. Stir and let simmer another 10 minutes. Add the cilantro and stir.

Stir diced mango into yogurt. Top each bowl of soup with a dollop of the mixture.

Yield: 6–8 servings

3 cups diced onion

3 tablespoons minced garlic

3 cups brown lentils

4 tablespoons canola oil

9 cups water

8 bay leaves

2 cans (13½ ounces each) coconut milk

4 teaspoons garam masala

3 tablespoons peeled and minced fresh gingerroot

Zest of 2 limes

¼ cup freshly squeezed lime juice

1 tablespoon and ½ teaspoon salt

2 tablespoons sugar or honey

1 cup cilantro leaves, packed

1 mango, peeled and diced

1 cup plain yogurt

Spicy Garbanzo-Tomato Soup

*I love to serve this soup with chopped avocado on top. With a
fresh, hot, crusty loaf of bread, it makes a meal.*

2 tablespoons minced garlic

2 cups diced onion

1 cup diced green bell pepper

4 tablespoons olive oil

4 cups canned Roma tomatoes in juice

1 (19-ounce) can garbanzo beans

3 tablespoons minced roasted Anaheim chiles

½ teaspoon salt

4 bay leaves

¼ teaspoon red pepper flakes

1½ teaspoons cumin

2 teaspoons chili powder

¼ cup minced fresh oregano

Splash of Tabasco

1 avocado, diced

In a heavy-bottomed 4-quart pot, sauté the garlic,
onion, and green bell peppers in the olive oil until
the onion becomes transparent. Add the tomatoes,
garbanzo beans, chiles, salt, bay leaves, red pepper
flakes, cumin, chili powder, oregano, and Tabasco.
Bring to a boil, turn down, and simmer for ½ hour.
Top each bowl with chopped avocado and serve.

Yield: 4–6 servings

Winter Seed and Squash Soup

When the rain is pouring down and the fire is lit, this soup warms the belly perfectly. The combination of seeds and nuts gives such weight and substance to the soup that it makes a satisfying meal in the dark of winter.

In a 3-quart soup pot, sauté the garlic, onion, and squash in the butter or oil until the onion becomes transparent. Add the tomatoes and water, cover, and bring to a boil. Turn down to low heat and simmer for 25 minutes.

Preheat oven to 350°F.

Toast the almonds on a small baking sheet for 8–10 minutes. Set aside to cool.

Meanwhile, toast the cumin and sesame seeds in a hot, dry skillet, stirring constantly, until they are golden brown. Grind the almonds, cumin, and sesame seeds all together in a food processor until they are smooth. Pour into a small bowl and set aside.

Blend the squash and tomato mixture in the food processor. Put back in the pot and return to the stove on low heat. Stir in the nut and seed mixture, chili powder, oregano, salt, sugar or honey, mushrooms, and cream. Serve immediately.

2 tablespoons minced garlic

2 cups diced onion

1 pound butternut squash, peeled and cubed

4 tablespoons butter or oil

4 cups diced Roma tomatoes

2 cups water

½ cup whole almonds

1 tablespoon whole cumin seed

⅓ cup whole sesame seeds

1 tablespoon chili powder

2 tablespoons minced fresh oregano

1 tablespoon salt

1 tablespoon sugar or honey

1 cup sliced meadow mushrooms

1 cup heavy cream

Note: This soup does not serve well after sitting long. The seeds and nuts expand in the liquid and the soup becomes too thick. If this does happen, add a little vegetable stock or water to thin it out.

Yield: 4 servings

Seared Pork Tenderloin with Spicy Green Apple–Tequila Sauce

This is a nice twist on the traditional combination of pork and apples.
The red pepper flakes and tequila add a "zing" to the dish. I serve it with polenta.

---

1 pound pork tenderloin, in one piece

1 teaspoon canola oil

½ cup Cafe Secret Sauce (p. 76)

2 cups Spicy Green Apple–Tequila Sauce (recipe follows)

3 cups Basic Polenta (p. 71)

Pull any fat or muscle fiber off the pork tenderloin. Slice on the diagonal into ¼-inch-thick pieces. Lay the pieces flat on your working surface. Hit each piece once with a meat mallet or the flat side of a broad knife. Set aside.

Lightly brush a large skillet with canola oil and put on high heat. When the oil is very hot, lay the pork slices in the skillet. When they start curling up at the sides (approximately 1 minute), flip, pour the Cafe Secret Sauce over (be careful—there will be a lot of hot steam and spray), cover, and turn off heat. Let sit for 1–2 minutes.

Pool ½ cup of the Spicy Green Apple–Tequila Sauce on each plate. Lay the tenderloin pieces on top of the sauce. Serve with Basic Polenta.

Yield: 4 servings

Spicy Green Apple—Tequila Sauce

This sauce is also outstanding with White Cheddar and Green Chile Tamales (p. 66) or Spicy Ancho Chile and Fresh Mozzarella Tamales (p. 28). Or, for a delicious lowfat meal, use it with a dense white fish or poultry.

In a heavy-bottomed 3-quart pot, cook the apples, apple juice, and water until the apples have broken down completely. Add the tequila, red pepper flakes, lemon zest and juice, cayenne, cumin, coriander, sugar, and salt.

Cook uncovered on low heat for 20 more minutes.

Storage: This sauce will keep in a tightly lidded container in the refrigerator for 7–10 days.

Yield: About 6 cups

5 large Granny Smith apples, peeled, cored, and cubed

2 cups apple juice

½ cup water

½ cup tequila

1 teaspoon red pepper flakes

Zest and juice of 2 lemons

⅛ teaspoon cayenne

¼ teaspoon ground cumin

¼ teaspoon ground coriander

½ cup and 2 tablespoons sugar

½ teaspoon salt

White Cheddar and Green Chile Tamales

Tamales are a festive, celebratory food. They look like little presents wrapped up and tied in cornhusks. You can keep them simple, or you can add any kind of cheese, chile, herb, or vegetable to the masa. You can even stuff the cornhusks with a bit of masa dough and steamed prawns or seared pork. Any way you prepare them, they are simply delicious.

18 cornhusks
¾ pound (3 sticks) unsalted butter
1½ teaspoons salt
1½ teaspoons baking powder
¾ cup milk
¾ cup whole corn kernels, fresh or fresh frozen
1½ cups masa harina
2 cups grated sharp white Cheddar cheese
1 cup diced roasted Anaheim chiles
Spicy Green Apple–Tequila Sauce (p. 65)

Soak the cornhusks in hot water to soften them while you are preparing the dough.

In a medium-sized mixing bowl, beat the butter, salt, and baking powder until light in color and doubled in size. Set aside. In a food processor, blend the milk and corn into a pulp. In another medium-sized mixing bowl, stir the milk and corn mixture into the masa until fully incorporated. Gradually add the masa mixture to the butter mixture, beating continuously until it is fully incorporated. Stir in the cheese and chiles. Using a ¼-cup scoop, divide the dough among 15 of the cornhusks. Wrap each husk around the dough. Tear the other 3 cornhusks into long strips to tie each end of the tamales.

On a rack in a steamer, cook for 10–12 minutes, covered, or until the tamales begin to ooze out of their wrappers a little bit. Serve immediately with Spicy Green Apple–Tequila Sauce.

Note: Tamale dough is very condusive to different kinds of spicing. Sometimes I add a cumin, chili powder, and cinnamon mixture to get a mole-type flavor. Other times, I add smoky chipotle chiles or fresh green herbs.

Yield: 15 tamales

Fresh Soba Noodles with Burdock Root, Ginger, and Wild Greens

*I grew up eating soba noodles, a pasta made with varying amounts of buckwheat
flour, sautéed with burdock. Burdock is an earthy root vegetable that has medicinal properties
as well as being delicious. You can probably find it in any Japanese market in your area. Soba
noodles are also available in Japanese markets and grocery stores with specialty food sections.
Try to find them fresh, if possible, as they are much lighter than the dried variety.*

Cook the soba noodles al dente according to package directions.

In a medium-sized skillet on high heat, sauté the garlic and onion in the sesame oil until the onion becomes transparent. Add the gingerroot and burdock, stirring on high heat for 1 minute. Add the bok choy, chard, and napa cabbage. Stir until the greens begin to wilt. Add the soba noodles and stir until the vegetables are evenly distributed throughout the noodles. Add the Cafe Secret Sauce and red pepper flakes, and stir for 1 more minute. Serve with the toasted sesame seeds sprinkled on top.

Note: If you can't readily find fresh soba noodles, you can substitute 4 ounces of dried soba in this recipe.

Yield: 2 servings

4 ounces fresh soba noodles

1 teaspoon minced garlic

½ cup diced onion

2 teaspoons light sesame oil or canola oil

1 teaspoon peeled and minced fresh gingerroot

¼ cup peeled and julienned burdock root

½ cup bok choy, cut on the diagonal

½ cup red chard, cut on the diagonal

½ cup thinly sliced napa cabbage

¼ cup Cafe Secret Sauce (p. 76)

⅛ teaspoon red pepper flakes (optional)

1 tablespoon sesame seeds, lightly toasted

Cafe Ten-Spice Chicken Sauté

Exotic in flavor, this is my version of a sweet-and-sour chicken.

1½ tablespoons minced garlic

¾ cup half-moon–shaped onion slices

2 tablespoons canola oil

5 ounces chicken breast, julienned

1 cup broccoli florets

20 snow peas

6 tablespoons Cafe Ten-Spice Marinade (recipe follows)

In a heavy-bottomed skillet on high heat, sauté the garlic and onion in the oil until the onion becomes transparent. Add the chicken strips and sauté for 1 minute. Add the broccoli and sauté 1 minute more. Add the snow peas and the Ten-Spice Marinade and toss until the chicken is just tender, approximately 3 more minutes. Serve on top of rice or fresh soba noodles.

Yield: 2 servings

SPICED NUTS

You can use either walnuts or pecans in this recipe. I have to hide these as soon as I make them or they will disappear very quickly. I put them on all of our dinner salads, with a leaf of Belgian endive.

¼ cup sugar

1 tablespoon minced orange zest

4 teaspoons curry powder

¼ teaspoon cayenne

1 teaspoon peeled and minced fresh gingerroot

3 tablespoons canola oil

2 cups whole shelled walnuts or pecans

Mix the sugar, orange zest, curry powder, cayenne, and gingerroot together in a small bowl. Set aside.

Place the canola oil in a large skillet on high heat. When it is very hot, add the nuts and stir constantly. Add the spice mixture 1 tablespoon at a time, continuing to stir until the mixture has caramelized. Pour the nuts onto a baking sheet to cool.

Storage: These nuts will keep in a tightly lidded container for up to 1 week.

Yield: 2 cups

Cafe Ten-Spice Marinade

*As you choose spices to mix, toast, and grind, consider the different countries
and regions from which these spices come and the endless combinations of flavor and
fragrance that proliferate around the world. I don't adhere to any strict theories about what
should or shouldn't go together, but I do follow my nose, literally—I smell the spices as
I toast them to see if they smell good together. I went to a restaurant one night for dinner
and enjoyed its "Five-Spice Chicken." When I decided to try my hand at my
own mix, I got rather enthusiastic and ended up at ten spices.*

*The uses for this marinade are similar to those for the Cafe Secret Sauce (p. 76).
I use it to marinate chicken, fish, or pork, but you can also sear meats, poultry, or fish in it.
I have also used this in rice dishes—sparingly, because the flavors are so strong.*

In a dry skillet on high heat, toast the coriander, cumin, fennel, mustard seed, and star anise, stirring constantly, until they are golden brown. Grind them to a fine powder with a mortar and pestle or in a small coffee or spice grinder.

Whisk all ingredients together.

Storage: This marinade will keep in a tightly lidded container in the refrigerator for up to 2 weeks.

Yield: About 2½ cups

1 teaspoon whole coriander seed

1 teaspoon whole cumin seed

1 teaspoon whole fennel seed

1 teaspoon whole black mustard seed

1 whole star anise

½ teaspoon ground cloves

1 teaspoon ground cinnamon

2 tablespoons peeled and minced fresh gingerroot

1 tablespoon minced garlic

1 tablespoon salt

⅓ cup brown sugar or honey

1 cup canola oil

1 cup seasoned rice vinegar

1 teaspoon red pepper flakes

Savory Polenta with Caponata and Fresh Mozzarella

You want to be really hungry when you eat this!
(For a lighter flavor, leave out the chocolate.)

---

2 tablespoons minced garlic

1 cup diced onion

½ cup high-quality olive oil

4 cups cubed, unpeeled eggplant

2 cups diced Roma tomatoes

¾ cup raisins

3 tablespoons capers

2 anchovies, minced

½ cup freshly squeezed lemon juice

1 tablespoon unsweetened chocolate, melted

1 cup minced parsley

2 teaspoons salt

Pepper

4 cups Basic Polenta (recipe follows)

4 ounces fresh mozzarella, sliced in ¼-inch rounds

In a small skillet on high heat, sauté the garlic and onion in the olive oil until the onion becomes transparent. Add the eggplant and sauté 1 more minute. Add the Roma tomatoes, raisins, capers, anchovies, and lemon juice, turn to low heat, and cook for 10 minutes, or until the eggplant is soft. Stir in the chocolate, parsley, salt, and pepper.

Place 1 cup of the polenta on each plate. With a spoon form an indentation in the middle of the polenta. Place one-quarter of the mozzarella in each indentation. Cover each serving with one-quarter of the caponata and serve.

Yield: 4 servings

Basic Polenta

Whenever I make polenta, everyone gathers around with little soup cups and spoons, asking me to "just dish up a little, please. . . ." Few foods are more comforting than a bowl of bright yellow, creamy, herbed polenta. In the cafe we use it in many ways. I add it to bread; I place it in tubs, refrigerate it, slice it, and grill it; I serve it sweet with honey and lemon, topping it off with mascarpone and berries; I serve it hot and savory with Cafe Roma Tomato Sauce (p. 75); or I use it as a crust for some savory baked dish. I even spread it out thin on a cookie sheet to cool, then use little star cookie cutters to make garnishes for soups. Polenta must take a bow: it is to be applauded as a supreme food.

In a large, heavy-bottomed soup pot, bring the water to a boil. Add the polenta in a thin stream, stirring constantly. When it begins to bubble, turn down to simmer, and stir occasionally to prevent sticking. Cook for 15 more minutes. Add the butter, olive oil, garlic, thyme, oregano, salt, lemon zest, and parsley. Cook for another 5 minutes and serve.

Storage: Cooked polenta will keep, tightly wrapped, in the refrigerator for up to 3 days.

Yield: 6 cups

6 cups water

2 cups raw polenta

2 tablespoons butter

2 tablespoons olive oil

1½ tablespoons minced garlic

1 teaspoon fresh thyme

2 tablespoons minced fresh oregano

2 teaspoons salt

Zest of 1 lemon

½ cup minced parsley

Confetti Ravioli with Carrot and Basil

This ravioli makes a beautiful presentation. The shreds of orange and green can be seen through the dough and hint at the holiday spirit.

16 ravioli squares (recipe for dough and cutting follows)

FILLING:

1 tablespoon minced garlic

1½ cups minced onion

2 tablespoons olive oil

1½ cups finely grated carrot

1 cup finely grated zucchini

1 cup finely chopped toasted walnuts

½ cup chopped basil

1 cup Montrachet cheese

1 cup grated Romano cheese

Pinch of fresh cracked pepper

Cafe Roma Tomato Sauce (p. 75) or *Savory Carrot-Thyme Tomato Sauce* (p. 32)

In a small skillet, sauté the garlic and onion in the olive oil until the onion becomes transparent.

In a large mixing bowl, combine all of the ingredients, including the sautéed onion and garlic, and mix until all of the vegetables and cheeses are evenly distributed.

Place ¼ cup of the filling in the middle of each 5-inch square of ravioli dough. Fold in half to form a triangle. Crimp the edges, being sure that there are no gaps in the crimping. Set aside, keeping covered with waxed paper or a light towel, until all of the ravioli are filled. At this point you may freeze the ravioli. Separate them with waxed paper and wrap airtight in plastic wrap. They will keep frozen for up to 1 month.

Put ½ teaspoon of salt in a large pot of boiling water. Drop the ravioli in the boiling water, four at a time, and cook for 8–10 minutes, or until the dough is al dente along the edges. Serve immediately in either Cafe Roma Tomato Sauce or Savory Carrot-Thyme Tomato Sauce.

Note: For an even more dramatic visual effect, try using finely grated beet along with the carrot and zucchini.

Yield: 4–5 servings (16 large ravioli)

Ravioli Dough

*I use this dough for all my ravioli recipes. You can use durum flour
for this dough, although it works well with unbleached white flour. It is a
very simple dough to make. I just put the flour directly on my work space, making a
well in the middle of it to pour the eggs in. After I make the ravioli, I boil up
the dough scraps to put in a soup—the different shapes look wonderful!*

Place your flour on any solid (immovable) work space. Make a well in the middle, and pour the beaten eggs into the well. Quickly begin scooping and molding the flour and eggs together so that the eggs don't run out. Continue molding in a circular motion with the palms of your hands, rather than your fingers, until you have a solid ball of dough. Knead for 8 more minutes, until the dough is smooth in texture.

> 4 cups flour
> 8 large eggs, beaten

Divide into four equal-sized balls. Roll each ball out as thin as you can in a square shape (approximately a 13-inch square), keeping a dusting of flour on the work surface so that the dough won't stick. Cut the square into four 5-inch squares to make four large ravioli. Repeat the process three more times, making 16 squares in all. At this point you can freeze the unfilled ravioli squares, separated with sheets of waxed paper and wrapped tightly in plastic wrap. They will keep for up to 1 month in the freezer.

Note: Extra ravioli dough can be rough-chopped into odd shapes and frozen to add later to soups.

Yield: 4–5 servings (16 large ravioli)

HOT POTATO CAESAR SALAD

I practically live on salads year-round, but in the wintertime the available organic greens never have the same flavor as in the summer. As the winds blew off Puget Sound and the fire burned in the little potbellied stove to keep us warm, our night cook, Anne, and I were trying to come up with a hot salad for our Valentine's Day dinner. We steamed off new potatoes and tossed them with a little Parmigiano-Reggiano, our Caesar Dressing, chives, and parsley.

4 cups cubed new potatoes
⅔ cup grated Parmigiano-Reggiano cheese
½ cup chopped parsley

½ cup chopped chives
½ cup Caesar Dressing (recipe follows)
Anchovies (optional)

Steam the cubed potatoes in a basket over boiling water for 12–15 minutes, or until tender. When the potatoes are cool, place them in a bowl and toss with the cheese, parsley, chives, and dressing. Serve immediately, garnished with anchovies.

Yield: 4–6 servings

CAESAR DRESSING

1 egg
1 tablespoon minced garlic
1 cup freshly squeezed lemon juice

1 teaspoon salt
½ teaspoon pepper
2 cups high-quality olive oil

Place the egg, garlic, lemon juice, salt, and pepper in a food processor and blend for 1 minute. Continue blending, adding the olive oil in a thin drizzle until the oil is fully combined.

Storage: This dressing will keep in a tightly lidded container in the refrigerator for up to 2 weeks.

Yield: About 3 cups

Cafe Roma Tomato Sauce

This is the basic red sauce that we use in various ways at the cafe. It is so versatile that it works as a pasta sauce, pizza sauce, under polenta, as a sauce to poach fish in (really good!), or even to bake eggs in for brunch. We make 3 gallons at a time.

In a heavy-bottomed saucepan on medium-high heat, sauté the garlic and onion in the olive oil until the onion becomes transparent. Add the red wine and cook for another 3 minutes. Add the tomatoes (being sure to break them up into small pieces), bay leaves, and herbs, and bring to a soft boil. Turn down to low and let simmer for ½ hour. Add the capers, honey, and salt. Either use immediately or refrigerate.

Storage: This sauce will keep in a tightly lidded container in the refrigerator for up to 1 week.

Yield: 4 cups

2 tablespoons minced garlic

2 cups finely diced onion

4 tablespoons high-quality olive oil

¾ cup hearty red wine

1 (28-ounce) can Roma tomatoes, including juice

3 bay leaves

⅓ cup finely chopped fresh herbs, packed (we use basil, oregano, marjoram, and/or thyme)

2 tablespoons capers

2 tablespoons honey

2 teaspoons salt

Cafe Secret Sauce

This sauce has many uses. I use it as a marinade for seafood, vegetables, and meat, especially when I want to grill them. Many recipes in this book that call for searing meat or seafood use this sauce. I have used it as a salad dressing for soba noodle and rice salads, and I use it in Fresh Soba Noodles with Burdock Root, Ginger, and Wild Greens (p. 67). When I make it, I prepare a large tub to use as I see fit, because it is very versatile and keeps well.

1 cup tamari
½ cup seasoned rice vinegar
½ cup dark toasted sesame oil
¼ cup minced fresh gingerroot
2 tablespoons minced garlic
¾ cup warm water
¼ cup brown sugar
½ teaspoon red pepper flakes

Whisk all ingredients together.

Storage: This sauce will keep in a tightly lidded container in the refrigerator for up to 3 weeks.

Yield: 3 cups

Cran-Tequila Sauce

I serve this with smoked trout or grilled dense white fish such as halibut.
It also makes a great sauce for roasted turkey.

In a 2-quart saucepan, bring all of the ingredients to a boil. Turn down to simmer until the cranberries completely break down, approximately 20 minutes.

Storage: This sauce will keep in a tightly lidded container in the refrigerator for up to 2 weeks.

Yield: About 2½ cups

1 (12-ounce) bag fresh cranberries

1 cup apple juice

½ cup tequila

½ cup sugar

Zest of 2 lemons

1 teaspoon minced garlic

1 tablespoon minced fresh rosemary

Chocolate Mousse Pie

If you like double-chocolate ice cream, this is the pie for you.

---

1 Chocolate Cookie Crumb Crust
(recipe follows)

FILLING:

6 tablespoons water

¾ cup sugar

2 cups heavy cream

7 egg yolks

1 whole egg

4 ounces bittersweet chocolate,
melted and cooled

1½ ounces unsweetened chocolate,
melted and cooled

Prepare the Chocolate Cookie Crumb Crust.

To make a simple syrup, simmer the water with the sugar until it is clear, approximately 4 minutes. Cover and remove from heat. Set aside.

With an electric mixer, whip the cream to soft-peak stage. Cover and refrigerate until you are ready to use it.

In a medium-sized mixing bowl, whip the egg yolks and the whole egg on high speed until light in color and frothy. While they are whipping, reheat the simple syrup to a rolling boil. Whipping on medium speed, gradually add the syrup to the eggs. Pour into a double boiler and, over simmering water, whisk for 5–7 minutes until thick and light in color. Return to the mixer and whip on medium speed for 5 minutes.

Put one-fourth of the melted cooled chocolate into a medium-sized mixing bowl. Add one-fourth of the whipped cream and whisk together briskly with a hand-held wire whisk. Quickly add and whisk in one-fourth of the egg mixture before the chocolate begins to harden. Repeat this process once more. Fold in the remaining ingredients.

Chill for 30 minutes in a bowl covered with plastic wrap and then pour into the Chocolate Cookie Crumb Crust.

Yield: One 9-inch pie

Chocolate Cookie Crumb Crust

We use this crust for the preceding Chocolate Mousse Pie, but you can also use it for a banana cream pie or any other cream pie filling that goes well with chocolate.

Preheat oven to 350°F.

On a baking sheet, toast the hazelnuts in the oven for 10–15 minutes. Roll in a towel to peel off the skins. Grind in a food processor.

Mix all ingredients together in a medium-sized bowl. Press into a 9-inch pie tin, being sure that the crust is evenly pressed over the bottom of the tin and up the sides.

Bake for 10–15 minutes. Let cool before filling.

Yield: One 9-inch pie crust

½ cup hazelnuts

1½ cups chocolate wafer crumbs

4 tablespoons brown sugar

7 tablespoons (⅞ stick) butter, melted and cooled

HOT MULLED WINE

The rain and clouds of November and December feel soft and comforting when you are sipping a mug of hot mulled wine by the fire. I offer this at the cafe all through the holiday season.

1½ liters hearty red wine	1 lime, sliced
4 cinnamon sticks	½ cup port
1 lemon, sliced	¼ cup tequila
1 orange, sliced	3 tablespoons sugar

Heat all ingredients slowly in a medium-sized pot to just below a simmer. Keep at very low heat for 1 hour. Do not boil. Turn off heat and serve.

Yield: about 2 quarts

SPRING

A Celebratory Spring Day

BREAKFAST:
Poppyseed-Lemon Scones and a steaming latte

LUNCH:
Smoked Salmon–Corn Cakes with Two-Squash Salsa and sour cream

DINNER:
Dilly Purple Cabbage Salad, Ahi Tuna Cakes with Green Onion,
Sesame, and Ginger

SPRING

SPRING IN THE PACIFIC NORTHWEST makes a premature entrance. I have lived here most of my life, yet every February still finds me exclaiming in surprise at the appearance of crocuses and daffodils with their bold purple and yellow coats, sometimes peeking through the snow. With this first sign of life, we start gathering large piles of fertilizer for the garden and feverishly reading through seed catalogs— and, in our excitement, we invariably spend three times what we had planned.

At the cafe, the gardens begin growing overnight, literally by inches, in about mid-March. Every morning brings us a new color, texture, smell, and birdsong as we drive in through the back gate. My delight in the season lets me procrastinate on the day's duties. Instead of making winter's quick dash from the car to the warmth and dryness inside, I meander through the garden, trying to remember the name of each new sprout. The 100-year-old pear tree stands over the garden with a grandfatherly, protective air. It has been transformed from its winter beauty—a textured etching against the gray skies and water—to a flurry of magnificent blossoms that the chinook winds blow around like snow outside the kitchen window. One morning I came around the corner and a young man was sitting peacefully in the arbor. I felt sorry to intrude, but I lived vicariously through the quiet picture of him all day.

We wait with eager anticipation at the cafe for the spring arrival of Rebecca's wild greens, which make up our daily salad mix from April to November. Although she waited tables for several years, Rebecca's true calling is gardening. Her salads are an experience for the eye as well as the palate, and tasting my way through them has been my education in wild greens. Honeysuckle, pansies, hollyhocks, and roses nestle in the garnishes on the plates. Leeks, sorrel, asparagus, chard, and bok choy dominate the menu until we relax, recognizing that they are not going away soon. The lunch board bears daily specials named for the season: "spring tart," "spring soup," "spring salad," and so on. We don't realize how far we've taken our spring frenzy until we put a lunch plate together and see that everything on it is green! Then we know it's time to branch out a little.

The first fresh halibut arrives from Alaska, and we excitedly begin braiding salmon and halibut together, having forgotten how exhausted we were by the end of the previous summer from weaving all those braids. But, all in all, spring brings a luscious rush of energy that breathes new life into the kitchen and renews our sense of Northwest abundance and well-being.

Smoked Salmon—Corn Cakes

I serve these cakes with Two-Squash Salsa (p. 111). I am sure there is no meal more representative of Northwest fare. The combination of corn (polenta in this version), smoked salmon, and summer squash brings the smell of saltwater and warm earth to the table, even if you are sitting in a high-rise apartment surrounded by concrete. If you are feeling really decadent, top the cakes with both the squash salsa and a little sour cream mixed with chives.

For the polenta: In a medium-sized, heavy-bottomed pot, bring the water, salt, garlic, and butter to a boil. Add the polenta in a thin stream, stirring constantly, until it boils again. Turn down to low, stirring occasionally to keep the polenta from sticking. Cook another 10–15 minutes and turn off.

For the corn cakes: Sift the flour, baking powder, baking soda, and salt into a large mixing bowl. Set aside.

In another large mixing bowl, whisk together the melted butter, eggs, buttermilk, and cooked polenta until completely mixed. Stir in the corn, salmon, parsley, chives, and green onions.

Make a well in the middle of the dry ingredients and pour the wet ingredients into the dry ingredients. Stir briskly until all ingredients are completely incorporated.

On medium-high heat, lightly coat a skillet with oil, and pour in ¼ cup of the batter per cake (an ice cream scoop works well for this). When the bottom edges turn golden brown and the top begins to bubble, flip. Turn heat to low and continue cooking until done. Serve immediately with Two-Squash Salsa.

Yield: 6–8 servings (about 24 cakes)

POLENTA:

2 cups water

⅔ teaspoon salt

2 teaspoons minced garlic

4 teaspoons butter

⅔ cup raw polenta

CORN CAKES:

1½ cups unbleached white flour

2¼ teaspoons baking powder

1½ teaspoons baking soda

¾ teaspoon salt

8 tablespoons (1 stick) butter, melted and cooled

4 eggs

2¼ cups buttermilk

2 cups whole corn kernels, fresh or frozen

1½ cups flaked smoked salmon

¾ cup chopped parsley

¼ cup chopped chives

1 cup chopped green onions

Canola oil for frying

Two-Squash Salsa (p. 111)

Mexican Cocoa Crepes with Ricotta-Orange Filling

I love the flavor of Mexican chocolate, so one day I decided to make a crepe with cocoa, cinnamon, a touch of nutmeg, and sugar. The spices lend themselves to many adaptations (try filling these crepes with fresh crabmeat and topping them with your favorite mole sauce!), but this sweet rendition is a cafe favorite.

CREPES:

1 cup unbleached white flour

3 tablespoons unsweetened cocoa powder

1 teaspoon cinnamon

¼ teaspoon grated fresh nutmeg

¼ teaspoon cardamom

½ teaspoon salt

4 eggs, beaten

1½ cups milk

3 tablespoons butter, melted

Butter for cooking the unfilled crepes

RICOTTA-ORANGE FILLING:

4 cups ricotta cheese

Zest of 2 oranges, minced

½ cup sugar

½ teaspoon cinnamon

½ cup bittersweet chocolate shards

Canola oil for frying the filled crepes

For the crepes: Sift together the flour, cocoa powder, cinnamon, nutmeg, cardamom, and salt into a small mixing bowl.

In a medium-sized bowl, whisk together the eggs, milk, and melted butter. Swiftly whisk in the flour and spice mixture until the consistency is creamy. Cover and refrigerate for 1 hour.

Lightly grease a crepe pan or a smooth-bottomed 10-inch skillet on medium heat. Pour approximately ¼ cup batter into the pan, being sure the batter covers the entire bottom. When the edges of the crepe begin to curl and pull away from the sides of the pan, flip the crepe. Cook another few seconds and remove from pan. Repeat until all of the crepes are cooked.

For the ricotta-orange filling: Mix all of the filling ingredients together in a medium-sized mixing bowl.

Place approximately ⅓ cup of the filling in the middle of each crepe. Fold the sides of the crepe over the filling. Bring the top and bottoms over the first fold. Place on a plate, folded side down, until you are ready to fry.

In a lightly oiled skillet, fry the filled crepes on both sides until golden brown. Serve immediately.

Note: Unfilled crepes can be kept in the refrigerator for up to 1 week, or in the freezer for up to 1 month. In either case, separate them with sheets of waxed paper and wrap the whole package tightly with plastic wrap.

Yield: 6 servings (about 12 crepes)

BREADS

Breads, like potatoes, rice, pasta, or eggs, beg to be transformed into any shape, flavor, or texture you can imagine. They can be a meal, an appetizer, the center of a dish, or merely the foundation for something bigger—the base for the meat in a sandwich, as it were. But fresh hot bread coming out of the oven dazzles the senses every time, whether it's a simple recipe or an extravagant one.

Whenever I begin making bread, I start by trying to think of a combination of flavors or a shape I haven't done before. (Boredom has a permanent seat at the table of creativity.) Sometimes I peruse my pantry shelves, waiting for an item to trigger an idea. Sometimes I look in the refrigerator for the same reason. I also use cookbook indexes daily to jog my brain into activity. I will go to "B" for breads and run down the list, hoping something will jump out.

At other times I already have the beginning of an idea. For instance I love sourdough so much that I wanted to try doing something more with it than simply making a plain baguette or loaf, so I added caramelized onion, fresh fennel, and fresh dill to the dough. Later, the fennel and dill triggered another idea. I love fennel with roasted vegetables, so I decided to stuff a bread dough with cheeses and roasted vegetables. This is how Wild Mushroom Braid with Herbs and Gruyère (p. 12) came about.

In general, when you are making yeasted breads, always mix the yeast with a little warm water first to be sure it is active. Let it stand long enough to bubble, and then you know it is okay to use. When adding flour, add a cup or two initially (depending on how much bread you are making) and then add a little more at a time (approximately 1/2 cup), working it in completely before adding more. This creates a smooth, elastic dough.

When putting a dough to rise, always be sure to cover it with a towel or plastic wrap. This keeps the top from drying out and stops it from cracking as it grows. Be patient: rising time varies greatly depending on what kind of dough you have made and how warm it is. In the winter our breads at the cafe can take all day to rise because our only heat is a little woodstove and our baking ovens.

Making bread takes very little actual "work" time. Mixing the dough might take 20 minutes, including kneading. Then the rest is rising and baking time. If you work at home, or if you are drawn to meditative activities, bread-making might be a lovely addition to your day.

Pakistani Home Fries

*One of our favorite breakfast-menu items at the cafe is a "home-fry sauté":
a filling plate of savory potatoes lightly sautéed with any vegetables we want to add,
melted sharp white Cheddar cheese, and one of our homemade salsas. Stephanie, our day
cook, suggested this curry idea as a twist on an old favorite: take the potatoes, make our own
curry, add spinach, tomatoes, and green onions, top with yogurt and Mango Chutney (p. 138)
or apple chutney (substitute apples for the mango in the Mango Chutney recipe), and
voilà! As with any curry, you can play with spices that please you until you come
up with your own version. I found that this dish is even better if you let the
potato-and-curry mixture meld overnight in the refrigerator.*

---

8 cups cubed, unpeeled potatoes

2 teaspoons salt

Zest of 1 lemon

1 cup cilantro leaves, packed

1 whole star anise

1 teaspoon whole cumin seed

1 teaspoon whole coriander seed

1 teaspoon whole black mustard seed

½ teaspoon whole fennel seed

1 teaspoon whole asafetida

1 tablespoon peeled and minced fresh gingerroot

1 tablespoon minced garlic

½ teaspoon ground cinnamon

½ teaspoon ground cloves

Pinch of cayenne

2 cups chopped green onion

2 cups diced fresh tomatoes

4 cups whole spinach leaves

1 cup plain yogurt

½ cup Mango Chutney (p. 138)

Steam the cubed potatoes in a basket over boiling water for 12–15 minutes or until tender. Cool slightly.

In a large mixing bowl, toss the potatoes with the salt, lemon zest, and cilantro. Set aside.

In a heavy-bottomed dry skillet on medium heat, toast the star anise, cumin, coriander, black mustard seed, fennel seed, and asafetida until lightly browned and aromatic. Grind with a mortar and pestle or in a small coffee or spice grinder. Add to the potatoes and toss until evenly distributed. Add the gingerroot, garlic, cinnamon, cloves, and cayenne. Toss again until evenly distributed. At this point you can cover and refrigerate the mixture until you are ready to use it.

Lightly oil a large, heavy-bottomed skillet on high heat. Sauté the green onion for 1 minute, then add the potato curry. Stir the potatoes until they are hot all the way through. Spread the tomatoes and spinach over the top, turn to low heat, and cover for 2 minutes, until the spinach wilts. Stir one more time to incorporate the tomato and spinach.

Serve immediately, topping each serving with ¼ cup yogurt and 2 tablespoons chutney.

Note: Asafetida powder is easier to find than whole (look in stores with specialty sections). Either way, the measurement works, you just get a fresher flavor.

If you enjoy this blend of spices, try using it in soups, sauces for seafood (or breading mixtures for seafood), poultry dishes, and rice (pilafs). I combine whole spices that I like, lightly toast them, and set them aside in an airtight jar in a cool, dark place to grind as I need them.

Yield: 4–6 servings

Hazelnut Waffles with Bittersweet Chocolate and Orange Whipped Cream

Why not have dessert for breakfast?

WAFFLES:

½ cup hazelnuts

2 cups unbleached white flour

2¼ teaspoons baking powder

1 teaspoon baking soda

½ teaspoon salt

½ cup finely chopped bittersweet chocolate

3 large eggs

5 tablespoons butter, melted and cooled

ORANGE WHIPPED CREAM:

1¾ cups buttermilk

1 cup heavy whipping cream

2 tablespoons sugar

Zest of 1 orange, minced

For the waffles: Preheat oven to 350°F. On a baking sheet, toast the hazelnuts in the oven for 10–15 minutes. Roll in a towel to peel off the skins. Grind in a food processor and set aside.

Heat up the waffle iron. In a medium-sized bowl, sift the flour, baking powder, baking soda, and salt. Stir in the hazelnuts and chocolate. Set aside.

Separate the eggs. In a medium-sized bowl, whisk the yolks until they turn a light yellow. Add the butter and buttermilk while continuing to whisk. Pour the dry ingredients into the wet ingredients, stirring constantly. Avoid overmixing.

With an electric mixer, beat the egg whites until they form stiff peaks. Fold them gently into the waffle batter.

For the orange whipped cream: With an electric mixer, whip the cream with the orange zest and sugar until it is stiff.

Grease the waffle iron. Pour ¾ cup batter for each waffle onto the waffle iron and cook for about 3 minutes.

Top each waffle with orange whipped cream and serve immediately.

Yield: Five 7-inch waffles

Savory Corn and Pepper Waffles

Although we call these "savory," they are really delicious with maple syrup. They are another example of a theme that runs through the food at the cafe, combining opposites: sweet and savory, sweet and sour, hot and cold, cooked and raw. At the cafe we offer these waffles with real maple syrup and a high-quality link sausage.

Heat up the waffle iron.

Sift together the flour, cornmeal, baking powder, baking soda, and salt into a large mixing bowl. Set aside.

Separate the eggs. In another large mixing bowl, whisk egg yolks until they turn a light yellow. Whisk in the butter and buttermilk. Stir in the chives, peppers, corn, and herbs.

With a large spoon or spatula, stir the wet ingredients into the dry ingredients until they are fully incorporated.

Beat the egg whites until they form stiff peaks. Gently fold them into the batter.

Grease the waffle iron. Pour ¾ cup batter for each waffle onto the waffle iron and cook for about 3 minutes. Serve.

Yield: Eight 7-inch waffles

3 cups unbleached white flour

2 cups cornmeal

5 teaspoons baking powder

1 tablespoon baking soda

1 teaspoon salt

7 large eggs

½ pound (2 sticks) butter, melted and cooled

4½ cups buttermilk

½ cup minced chives

⅔ cup minced red and green bell peppers

⅔ cup corn kernels

¼ cup minced fresh herbs (we use Greek oregano, thyme, and parsley)

Kingston Scones

We make scones every morning at the cafe. We have a basic recipe that we mix ahead of time. Each morning we get to decide what flavors appeal to us. Savory, sweet, berry-filled, jam-filled—any way you fix them, these scones are warm and delicious.

2½ cups unbleached white flour

2½ cups cake flour

9 tablespoons sugar

1 teaspoon baking soda

1½ teaspoons baking powder

1 teaspoon cream of tartar

¾ teaspoon salt

¾ pound plus 2 tablespoons (3¼ sticks) cold unsalted butter

½ cup cold buttermilk plus additional if needed

½ cup heavy cream

1 egg, beaten

In making scones, there are a few basic rules to follow:

1. Keep the butter and the liquids very cold.

2. Don't overmix when adding the butter or the liquid; the dry mix should resemble pie dough before the liquid is added.

3. Don't overbake! I remove them from the oven when the bottoms have turned light brown. Jeannie, our baker, says, "When in doubt, pull them out!"

Preheat oven to 425°F.

Sift together the flours, sugar, soda, baking powder, cream of tartar, and salt into a medium-sized mixing bowl. Set aside.

Cut the butter into ½-inch pieces.

With an electric mixer on low speed, add butter 2 to 3 tablespoons at a time to the dry ingredients until it is fully incorporated, approximately 3–5 minutes in all. At this point, the mix can be refrigerated for up to 3 days, or frozen for up to 1 month, and used as needed. (It must be brought to room temperature before the wet mix is added.)

In a small mixing bowl, whisk together the buttermilk, cream, and beaten egg.

Pour the cream and egg mixture in a thin, steady stream into the butter and flour mixture, while mixing continuously with a fork. The dough should be just wet enough to hold together when you press it together. Add any optional ingredients (see Note).

Divide the dough into 12 equal portions, shape into balls, and gently press flat. Place on a greased baking sheet and bake for 5 minutes. Turn the oven down to 350°F and bake for another 10–15 minutes, until the bottoms are golden brown and the tops are a light golden color.

Note: When you add extra ingredients and flavors to scones, the dough may need a little more or less buttermilk to hold together. It's also important *when* you add the extra ingredients: Add ingredients such as fresh gingerroot and poppyseeds to the wet mix. Add citrus zest, chocolate shards, fruit (fresh, frozen, or dried), herbs, and cheeses to the dry mix *after* the sugars and fats have been incorporated but *before* the wet mix is added.

To make jam-filled scones, finish the scones to the point of having them molded and on the baking sheet. With the bottom of a soup spoon, press an indentation into the middle of each scone. Place 1 tablespoon of jam in each indentation.

Yield: 12 scones

SOME OF OUR FAVORITE SCONE VARIATIONS:

- 2 tablespoons peeled and grated fresh gingerroot and 1½ cups grated coconut
- Zest of 1 orange, minced, and 1 cup slivered bittersweet chocolate
- Zest of 1 orange, minced, and ⅔ cup each slivered bittersweet chocolate and toasted, ground hazelnuts
- Zest of 1 orange, minced, and 1 cup dried cranberries
- Zest of 1 orange, minced, and 1 cup slivered dried apricots
- ⅔ cup chopped dates and ⅔ cup chopped walnuts
- 2 tablespoons minced lemon zest and ⅓ cup poppyseeds
- 2 tablespoons minced lemon zest and 1 cup currants
- 1 tablespoon minced lemon zest and ¾ cup slivered candied ginger
- 2 tablespoons minced lemon zest and 1 tablespoon (per scone) of raspberry jam
- 2 cups fresh or frozen blueberries and 1 teaspoon almond extract

Potato-Tarragon Pancakes

Many of our community celebrations are centered on birthdays (one of the first honorees having been born right in my bed!), other momentous occasions, and rites of passage. Often the focus of the gathering seems to be the planning of the meal, which is often a potluck. Potato pancakes (or latkes, in traditional Jewish gatherings) are as irresistible as potato chips: one is never enough. Whether you use tarragon, as I have suggested in this recipe, or other fresh herbs, these pancakes will keep people coming back to the table.

4 medium red potatoes

2 tablespoons minced garlic

2 cups minced onion

2 tablespoons butter

2 tablespoons canola oil

2 cups milk

4 eggs

2 tablespoons minced fresh tarragon

½ cup minced chives

½ teaspoon black pepper

2 teaspoons salt

1 cup flour

1 teaspoon baking powder

1 cup freshly grated Parmesan cheese

1 cup chopped fresh parsley

Quince Purée (p. 15) or *Spicy Green Apple–Tequila Sauce* (p. 65)

Steam the potatoes whole for 30 minutes. Peel and grate them coarsely.

In a large skillet, sauté the garlic and onion in the butter and oil. In a medium-sized bowl, whisk the milk and eggs together. Add the grated potato, tarragon, chives, pepper, and salt, and then the sautéed garlic and onion.

Sift the flour and baking powder together into a large bowl. Stir in the Parmesan cheese and parsley. Pour the wet ingredients into the dry ingredients and stir thoroughly.

Cook the pancakes on medium-high heat in a lightly oiled skillet. Use a ¼-cup scoop to pour the batter into the pan. When they start crusting around the edge (about 3 minutes), flip. Cook another 3 minutes. They should be golden brown on both sides.

Note: This batter does not hold well. Once you have made it, cook the pancakes and eat them! I have served these with both Quince Purée and Spicy Green Apple–Tequila Sauce— either way, they're delicious.

Yield: 4–6 servings (about 12–15 medium-sized pancakes)

Lentil, Swiss Chard, and Lemon Soup

Quite a few greens can survive a Northwest winter and come on even stronger in spring. Swiss chard, sorrel, and kale are in our little garden behind the cafe kitchen, to grab year-round whenever we need a splash of green in a dish.

Although I often think of beans as a dead-of-winter, stick-to-your-ribs ingredient, lentils mixed with young Swiss chard leaves and the lightness of lemon fend off the chill of a Northwest spring day without feeling too heavy.

In a medium-sized, heavy-bottomed pot, sauté the garlic, onion, and lentils in the olive oil for 3 minutes on high heat. Add the bay leaves and water or stock. Cover and bring to a boil. Turn down to simmer for 40 minutes. Add the Swiss chard, thyme, lemon zest, ½ cup of the lemon juice, salt, and 2 teaspoons of the honey. Cook for another 10 minutes.

Meanwhile, dissolve the remaining 1 teaspoon of honey in the remaining ¼ cup of lemon juice and stir into the yogurt.

Serve the soup with a dollop of the yogurt mixture in each bowl.

Yield: 4–6 servings

2 tablespoons minced garlic

2 cups diced onion

2 cups brown lentils

¼ cup olive oil

4 bay leaves

7 cups water or vegetable stock

4 cups thinly sliced Swiss chard

1 tablespoon fresh thyme

Zest of 1 lemon

¾ cup freshly squeezed lemon juice

2½ teaspoons salt

3 teaspoons honey

¾ cup yogurt

Potato, Sorrel, and Nettle Soup

*Nettles are a nightmare for Northwest berry pickers and mushroom hunters.
They seem to grow everywhere, and they sting with the slightest touch. (The sting goes
away when you cook them, though. And they are particularly high in Vitamins A and C and
iron.) Wear rubber gloves to gather them so you don't get stung. Pick small, young shoots,
not more than 6 inches tall, in early spring. They are delicious and nutritious!*

1 tablespoon minced garlic

2 cups diced onion

4 cups unpeeled, cubed potatoes

4 tablespoons canola oil

4 cups water

1 cup chopped sorrel leaves, packed

1 cup chopped nettle leaves, packed

2 teaspoons salt

½ teaspoon pepper

Zest of 1 lemon

1 tablespoon minced fresh dill

⅔ cup cream

In a medium-sized soup pot, sauté the garlic, onion, and potato in the oil until the potato becomes transparent. Add the water, cover, and bring to a boil. Turn down to low and simmer for 30 minutes.

Blend half of the potato mixture to a smooth purée and return to the pot. Add the sorrel, nettles, salt, pepper, lemon zest, dill, and cream. Heat but do not boil.

Note: Do not pick nettles along heavily traveled roads. Many roadsides are regularly sprayed with herbicides.

Yield: 4 servings

Pear-Ginger Soup

This soup is great hot or cold.

In a heavy-bottomed 4-quart pot, sauté the garlic, onion, gingerroot, and pears in the butter or oil until the onion becomes transparent. Add the apple juice and water. Bring to a boil, turn to low heat, and simmer for 25 minutes or until the pears are completely broken down.

Meanwhile, in a dry skillet on high heat, toast the coriander, cumin, and cardamom seeds until golden brown. Grind them with a mortar and pestle or in a coffee or spice grinder. Set aside.

Blend the cooked pear mixture in a food processor until perfectly smooth. Put back into the soup pot and return to the stove on low heat. Add the coriander, cumin, cardamom, cayenne, cloves, curry powder, cinnamon, salt, sugar or honey, lemon zest, lemon juice, and cream or yogurt. Heat gently but do not boil. Serve immediately.

Yield: 4 servings

2 tablespoons minced garlic

2½ cups minced onion

2 tablespoons peeled and minced fresh gingerroot

6 cups unpeeled, diced Anjou pears

4 tablespoons butter or canola oil

2 cups apple juice

1 cup water

1 teaspoon whole coriander seed

½ teaspoon whole cumin seed

¼ teaspoon whole cardamom seed

Pinch of cayenne

¼ teaspoon ground cloves

1 teaspoon curry powder

½ teaspoon ground cinnamon

2½ teaspoons salt

2½ tablespoons sugar or honey

Zest and juice of 2 lemons

2 cups cream or yogurt

Thai Snow Pea and Prawn Soup with Red Rice

*Joe and Sandy are two patrons who have been coming in since
we opened in 1993. Sandy is a tall, intelligent, beautiful brunette who attracts
a lot of interest because she is a private detective. Over a glass of her favorite wine,
she tells us tales of hanging out in parks, nonchalantly refusing to carry a gun. Joe, who grew
up in Taiwan, travels a great deal for his work. He also loves to cook, and his travels are woven
into the meals that come out of his kitchen. He described a soup that he had enjoyed in
Hawaii with these ingredients. The visual effect is stunning—the light broth with
little green specks of cilantro on top, the red rice, and the pink prawns. Be sure
to start cooking the Red Rice well in advance—it takes a long time.*

2 tablespoons minced garlic

⅓ cup peeled and minced fresh gingerroot

4 cups diced onion

¼ cup canola oil

3 cups chicken or vegetable stock

2 cups canned, unsweetened coconut milk

1 stalk fresh lemongrass, chopped, or 1 tablespoon dried

12 snow peas

12 prawns, peeled and deveined

Zest of 2 limes

⅓ cup freshly squeezed lime juice

¼ teaspoon red pepper flakes, or ½ teaspoon minced fresh jalapeño

1½ teaspoons salt

7 teaspoons sugar

1 cup cilantro leaves, packed

1 recipe Red Rice (recipe follows)

In a medium-sized, heavy-bottomed pot on high heat, sauté the garlic, gingerroot, and onion in the oil until the onion becomes transparent. Add the chicken or vegetable stock, coconut milk, and lemongrass and bring to a boil. Cover, turn down to low, and simmer for 20 minutes.

Meanwhile, lightly steam the snow peas for 2–3 minutes and keep warm. In a separate utensil, lightly steam the prawns until they turn pink (approximately 3 minutes) and keep warm.

Add the lime zest and juice, red pepper flakes or jalapeño, salt, sugar, and cilantro to the soup. Divide soup among six bowls, place a scoop of Red Rice in the middle of each, and surround rice with 2 snow peas and 2 prawns. Serve immediately.

Note: The cilantro must be added just before serving. It loses its fresh flavor if cooked for long. I usually add it, turn off the heat, and serve the soup immediately.

Yield: 6 servings

Red Rice

There are many different kinds of red rice. They vary in price and flavor, but all are fun to work with. When I first made this rice I was naively expecting a quick, basmati-type finish. Two hours later, the rice still was not done, and I realized I was dealing with something very different. For this recipe I use a Thai red rice that has a chewy texture when done. It is a deep brick red color with a white interior and lots of flavor.

On medium heat, in a medium-sized, heavy-bottomed pot, sauté the garlic and onion in the oil until the onion becomes transparent. Add the rice and sauté another 3 minutes. Add the chicken stock, water, salt, and lemon zest. Cover and bring to a boil. Turn down to low and cook for another 2½ hours.

Yield: About 4 cups

1 tablespoon minced garlic
1 cup finely diced onion
1 tablespoon canola oil
1½ cups raw red rice
2 cups chicken stock
1 cup water
½ teaspoon salt
Zest of 1 lemon

DILLY PURPLE CABBAGE SALAD

Before all of the color comes on full in our spring gardens (and in the produce section of our refrigerator), we make this salad as a condiment to liven up our plates. The purple becomes even more brilliant when the cabbage is lightly tossed with the rice vinegar and oil.

3 cups purple cabbage, sliced paper-thin
½ cup seasoned rice vinegar
¼ cup canola oil

2 teaspoons minced fresh dill
1 tablespoon minced garlic
½ teaspoon salt
½ teaspoon sugar

Toss all ingredients together in a medium-sized mixing bowl. Serve immediately.

Yield: About 3 cups

Mexican Chicken Soup

I get big, beautiful, free-range, organic chickens from a man in Kingston. He just showed up at the back door one day, quietly making an offer I couldn't refuse. I get 50 or 60 at a time, smoke some of them, and freeze the rest. If you don't have the time to make a traditional stock, this is a quick and easy way to make chicken soup. It is delicious on its own, and with guacamole and chips on top, it can be a meal.

2 tablespoons minced garlic

2 cups diced onion

2 cups diced green and red bell peppers

2 tablespoons canola oil

1 pound boneless chicken breast, cubed

8 cups water

1 bay leaf

¾ teaspoon red pepper flakes

2 teaspoons ground cumin

2 tablespoons chopped fresh oregano

½ cup chopped parsley

2 teaspoons salt

In a large soup pot on high heat, sauté the garlic, onion, and peppers in the oil until the onion becomes transparent. Add the cubed chicken breast and stir for 1 more minute. Add the water and bay leaf, cover, and bring to a boil. Turn down to low and simmer for 30–45 minutes.

Stir in the red pepper flakes, cumin, oregano, parsley, and salt. Serve

Yield: 4–6 servings

Fettuccine with Oysters, Spinach, Pernod, and Gruyère

This combination began with the traditional dish Oysters Rockefeller.
You bake the oysters with spinach, Pernod (a licorice-flavored liqueur), and Gruyère.
So I thought, "Why not a pasta?"

In a large pot of boiling water, cook fettuccine al dente according to package directions.

Meanwhile, in a medium-sized skillet on high heat, sauté the garlic and onion in the oil until the onion becomes transparent. Add the oysters, spinach, and Pernod, turn down to low, and cover until the spinach wilts. Add the fettucine, cream, fennel seed, and Gruyère and stir continuously until the cheese is evenly melted and creates a sauce with the cream. Stir in the lemon zest, salt, and pepper to taste. Serve.

Yield: 2 servings

8 ounces fettuccine
2 tablespoons minced garlic
1 cup diced onion
4 tablespoons canola oil
10 small to medium oysters
2 cups spinach leaves, packed
6 tablespoons Pernod
⅔ cup cream
1 teaspoon whole fennel seed
1 cup grated Gruyère cheese
2 teaspoons lemon zest
¼ teaspoon salt
Pepper

Risotto with Rock Shrimp and Spinach in Coconut-Curry-Lime Sauce

Amel and Janice, who live in the Port Townsend area, deliver all of our seafood (still alive!) to the kitchen door. They raise divine Mediterranean mussels on their property, and their neighbors raise oysters. When Amel brought these juicy warm-water shrimp to me from the Gulf Coast, I had never tasted them before, and I was thoroughly entranced. These morsels are very rich in flavor and a little crisp in texture, with lots of juice.

---

2 tablespoons butter

1 tablespoon minced garlic

½ cup diced onion

4 cups cooked Basic Risotto (p. 25)

2¼ cups Coconut-Curry-Lime Sauce (recipe follows)

1 cup rock shrimp

2 cups spinach leaves, packed

4 teaspoons sugar

1 teaspoon salt

In a smooth-bottomed skillet on high heat, melt the butter. Sauté the garlic and onion until the onion is transparent. Add the risotto and the Coconut-Curry-Lime Sauce. Stir until the sauce is fully integrated. Turn to medium heat and add the shrimp and spinach. Cover to let the spinach wilt. When the shrimp have turned pink, stir in the sugar and salt. Serve immediately.

Yield: 2 servings

Coconut-Curry-Lime Sauce

Sometimes I think I would be quite content to limit myself to this combination of flavors; lime, spices, and coconut marry so well that satisfaction is always within easy grasp. I use this sauce with pasta dishes (Asian rice noodles are lovely) or rice dishes, as well as with the preceding risotto. Like other curries, the spice blend itself can be added to soups and legumes. Just toast up the whole spices and keep them tightly covered until you are ready to use them (they can hold for up to 1 month this way). Grind only the amount you wish to use.

In a small, dry skillet on high heat, toast the coriander, cumin, star anise, mustard seed, and fennel seed until lightly browned and aromatic. Grind them with a mortar and pestle or in a small coffee or spice grinder.

In a large bowl, whisk all of the ingredients together until well blended.

Storage: This sauce will keep in a tightly lidded container in the refrigerator for up to 3 days.

Yield: 4½ cups

2 teaspoons whole coriander seed

1 teaspoon whole cumin seed

1 star anise

½ teaspoon whole black mustard seed

1 teaspoon whole fennel seed

Zest and juice of 4 limes

2 (14-ounce) cans unsweetened coconut milk

⅛ teaspoon red pepper flakes

1½ teaspoons turmeric

⅛ teaspoon cayenne

1 teaspoon ground cinnamon

¼ teaspoon ground cloves

¼ cup and 2 teaspoons sugar

1 tablespoon salt

Fresh Soba Noodles with Green Mango and Cilantro

This dish was born when I ordered mangoes for the cafe and received a box of hard green fruit. The next day I was trying to think of different ingredients to go with soba noodles, and for some reason green mango sounded good to me. I pulled one of the fruits out of the box, peeled it, and tasted it. The flavor is delicious, tart, and crisp, with just a hint of sweetness to come.

8 ounces fresh soba noodles

2 teaspoons minced garlic

1 cup diced onion

2 teaspoons peeled and minced fresh gingerroot

4 teaspoons light sesame oil

1 cup green mango strips

1 cup red chard, sliced on the diagonal

1 cup bok choy, sliced on the diagonal

1 cup cilantro leaves, packed

½ cup Cafe Secret Sauce (p. 76)

½ cup cashews, lightly toasted

Cook soba noodles al dente according to package directions.

In a large skillet on high heat, sauté the garlic, onion, and gingerroot in the sesame oil until the onion becomes transparent. Add the mango, red chard, and bok choy, stirring for 1 more minute or until the chard begins to wilt. Add the soba noodles and stir, making sure the vegetables get evenly distributed. Stir in the cilantro and the Cafe Secret Sauce just to heat through. Serve immediately, topped with the cashews.

Note: Fresh soba noodles are incomparably better than dried ones. You can find them in grocery stores with specialty food sections or in Japanese/Asian markets. If you can't readily find fresh noodles, you can substitute 8 ounces of dried soba in this recipe.

Yield: 2 servings

Angel Hair Pasta with Leeks, Asparagus, and Portobello Mushrooms

*After a winter of heavier pasta dishes, I hunger for
lighter fare when I see the first crocuses and daffodils coming up.*

*Baby asparagus and leeks come into the market, welcomed by a frenzied
mass of customers looking for tastes that remind them of the spring garden.
With such delicate flavors, there is no need for heavy sauces or cream.*

Cook pasta al dente according to package directions.

In a large skillet on high heat, sauté the garlic and leeks in the olive oil for 1 minute. Add the asparagus tips and mushrooms and stir for 1 more minute. Add the pasta, herbs, and sherry, stirring to distribute the vegetables throughout the pasta. Stir in the cheese, lemon zest, red pepper flakes, and parsley. Salt to taste. Serve.

Yield: 2 large servings

8 ounces angel hair pasta

2 tablespoons minced garlic

1 cup leeks, sliced on the diagonal ⅛ inch thick

4 tablespoons olive oil

1 cup asparagus tips (1 inch long)

1½ cups sliced portobello mushrooms

2 tablespoons fresh herbs (we use basil, oregano, dill, and chervil)

5 tablespoons sherry

½ cup grated pecorino Romano cheese

2 teaspoons lemon zest

¼ teaspoon red pepper flakes (optional)

½ cup chopped parsley

Salt

COUSCOUS SALAD

This salad can be either a side dish with a meal or a meal in itself.

2 cups water

1½ cups raw couscous

1 cup minced parsley, packed

1 cup finely chopped green onions (both white and green parts)

1 cup chopped toasted almonds

1 cup currants

½ cup frozen peas (optional)

1½ cups Orange-Cinnamon-Curry Dressing (p. 110)

½ teaspoon salt

½ cup seasoned rice vinegar plus more as needed if the couscous sits (see Note)

In a small saucepan, bring the water to a boil. Add the couscous, cover, turn the heat off, and let sit, covered, for 10 minutes. Turn into a bowl and let cool.

Toss all ingredients in a medium-sized mixing bowl and serve.

Note: Couscous soaks up dressing. If this salad is to sit for longer than half an hour or so, it will tend to dry out, and you will probably need to splash in more seasoned rice vinegar (perhaps ¼ cup) to "wet" it again. However, this trick always works, so if you want to make this salad the day before and keep it refrigerated, just keep in mind that you will need to re-dress it before serving.

For a delightful variation, try substituting thinly sliced dried apricots for the currants in this recipe.

Yield: 6 servings

Ahi Tuna Cakes with Green Onion, Sesame, and Ginger

These are much lighter in flavor than the Fresh Yellowfin Tuna Cakes (p. 132).
The Cafe Secret Sauce, combined with the green onion and sesame seeds, gives these
an Oriental flavor. I serve them with Dilled Cucumber Salad (p. 137).

Preheat oven to 375°F.

Drizzle the ahi fillets with the 2 tablespoons of Cafe Secret Sauce and bake for 8–10 minutes. Cool and flake.

In a medium-sized mixing bowl, combine the fish with the rest of the ingredients, including the remaining ⅓ cup of Cafe Secret Sauce. Divide into 10 cakes. At this point you can refrigerate them, covered, for up to 24 hours.

In a lightly oiled, smooth, nonstick skillet on medium-high heat, fry the cakes until golden brown on one side, approximately 3 minutes. Flip and fry on the other side until golden brown. Serve immediately.

Yield: 5 servings (10 cakes)

1 pound ahi tuna fillets

2 tablespoons plus ⅓ cup Cafe Secret Sauce (p. 76)

2 eggs, beaten

1 cup chopped cilantro leaves

1 cup finely chopped green onion (both white and green parts)

⅓ cup sesame seeds, lightly toasted

½ cup dry bread crumbs

Parsnip-Coconut Cakes with Seared Salmon

Although parsnips are an autumn harvest item, every time I make these cakes I think of Easter and spring—why? I think the lightness of the cakes mixed with the aroma of coconut somehow reminds me of those spongy, coconut-covered Easter eggs that greet you at every checkout counter in every store around Easter time. Although I have never tasted those, I am convinced that these cakes are probably much better.

4 egg yolks

4 cups finely diced parsnips

1 (13½-ounce) can unsweetened coconut milk

½ cup unbleached white flour

1 teaspoon baking powder

1 tablespoon sugar

1 teaspoon salt

Pinch of cayenne

Light oil for searing the salmon

5 salmon fillets, about 5 ounces each

½ cup Cafe Secret Sauce (p. 76)

In a food processor, blend the egg yolks for 1 minute. Add the parsnips, coconut milk, flour, baking powder, sugar, salt, and cayenne and blend until smooth. Refrigerate for ½ hour.

Lightly oil a medium-sized skillet. Scoop the batter into the skillet, using a 4-ounce ice cream scoop for each cake. Cook cakes on medium-high heat for 3–4 minutes until golden brown. You will need a stiff (metal) pancake turner to flip the cakes (gently!). Cook for another 3–4 minutes and keep warm while you cook the salmon.

Lightly oil a nonstick skillet on high heat. When the oil is hot, place the salmon fillets in the pan (you should hear loud sizzling!). Cook for 2–3 minutes, flip, add the Cafe Secret Sauce, cover immediately, and turn off. Let sit for another minute and serve immediately.

Storage: The batter for the Parsnip-Coconut Cakes will keep in a tightly lidded container in the refrigerator for up to 1 week.

Yield: 5 servings (Fifteen 3-inch cakes)

Lemony Sorrel and Spinach Sauce

This sauce is especially delicious with poached salmon, although in our kitchen we also just pour it over rice, smear it on a fresh baguette, dip vegetables in it— any way to get it into our mouths goes. I make buckets of it because the sorrel in the back garden gets so out of hand and I can't bear to waste it.

In a food processor blend for 1 minute the egg, egg yolk, lemon zest, lemon juice, rice vinegar, tarragon, salt, garlic, sugar, sorrel, and spinach. With the food processor running, drizzle the canola oil in a thin stream into the spinach mixture.

Note: This sauce is also delicious made with all sorrel rather than a combination of sorrel and spinach.

Storage: This sauce will keep in a tightly lidded container in the refrigerator for up to 1 week.

Yield: 6 cups

1 whole egg
1 egg yolk
Zest of 2 lemons
½ cup freshly squeezed lemon juice
1 cup seasoned rice vinegar
¼ cup tarragon leaves
1 teaspoon salt
1½ tablespoons minced garlic
1 tablespoon sugar
1 cup sorrel leaves
1 cup spinach leaves
4½ cups canola oil

ORANGE-CINNAMON-CURRY DRESSING

This dressing has robust flavors. As with many items in this book, I make a couple of quarts at a time and have it around to use when the mood strikes. I have used this with green salads and rice salads as well as with the Couscous Salad (p. 106).

1 cup seasoned rice vinegar
2 tablespoons minced garlic
2 teaspoons cinnamon
2 teaspoons curry powder

2 tablespoons minced orange zest
½ teaspoon salt
1 tablespoon sugar or honey
2 cups canola oil

In a blender or food processor, blend all of the ingredients except the oil for 1 minute. Continuing to blend, gradually add the oil in a thin drizzle. The dressing will thicken.

Storage: This dressing will keep in a tightly lidded container in the refrigerator for up to 2 weeks.

Yield: About 3 cups

Two-Squash Salsa

I use Two-Squash Salsa with many menu items. The red, green, and yellow of the squash and peppers look almost like confetti, and the flavors liven up many a simple dish. Sometimes this salsa accents a soup perfectly—I have garnished Lentil-Tomato Harvest Soup (p. 19) with it, or Black Bean, Lime, and Chile Soup (p. 60)—or it can top summer frittatas (any kind of eggs and herbs or cheeses with this salsa is great). Blackened fish, chicken, or summer rice dishes also work very well with this salsa.

In a medium-sized bowl, lightly stir all ingredients together. This sauce does not keep well, so serve it immediately, or cover, refrigerate, and use it within 24 hours.

Yield: About 3 cups

1 cup minced zucchini

1 cup minced crookneck squash

1 cup chopped green onion

1 cup minced red bell pepper

Zest of 2 limes

⅓ cup freshly squeezed lime juice

⅔ cup roughly chopped cilantro

3 tablespoons minced fresh oregano

1 teaspoon salt

2½ tablespoons sugar

Generous pinch of cayenne

Papaya–Red Pepper Salsa

I love to serve this salsa in the spring, when everyone is not-so-patiently waiting for summer to be here. I use it with oysters, halibut, scallops, frittatas, and any bean/rice platter that needs a little dressing up. The combination of peppers and sweet papaya allows all of us to happily pull out our last reserves of patience.

2 cups peeled and diced papaya

¼ cup minced red bell peppers

Zest of 2 limes

⅓ cup freshly squeezed lime juice

¼ cup finely chopped green onion

½ cup roughly chopped cilantro

⅛ teaspoon cayenne, or 1 teaspoon minced fresh jalapeño

4 teaspoons sugar

1 teaspoon salt

Mix all ingredients together in a stainless steel or glass bowl. Serve immediately. This salsa does not last well—the cilantro loses its freshness after 3–4 hours.

Note: Papayas, like all fruits, can vary in sweetness. For some guidelines on balancing this and other fresh fruit sauces, see "Salsas and Chutneys," p. 31.

Yield: About 3 cups

Lemon Meringue Pie

For me, making a lemon meringue pie is the quintessential quest for perfection.
This is the closest we've come.

Preheat oven to 350°F.

For the filling: In a medium-sized bowl, mix the sugar, cake flour, cornstarch, and salt.

In a heavy-bottomed stainless steel pan, bring the water, ¼ cup of the lemon juice, and the sugar mixture to a boil. Turn the heat to medium and whisk for 5–7 minutes, or until the mixture becomes thick and translucent.

In a medium-sized mixing bowl, whisk the egg yolks and the whole egg together. Pour one-third of the hot lemon mixture into the eggs, whisk, and pour back into the pan. Continue whisking the mixture for 5 more minutes, or until it thickens and lightens in color. Remove from heat, add the butter and stir until it melts. Whisk in the remaining lemon juice. Pour into the prebaked pie shell.

For the meringue: In a large mixing bowl, whip the egg whites on high speed until frothy. Continuing to whip, add the cream of tartar and then the sugar, 1 tablespoon at a time. Whip until the whites form stiff, glossy peaks.

Mound the meringue onto the lemon filling in the pie shell. Spread to seal the edges. Bake for approximately 15 minutes, or until the tips of the meringue are a light brown. Chill overnight.

Yield: One 9-inch pie

---

1 prebaked, fluted 9-inch pie shell (see Basic Pie Crust, p. 148)

FILLING:

1 cup and 1 tablespoon sugar

2 tablespoons cake flour

2 tablespoons cornstarch

¼ teaspoon salt

1¼ cups water

¾ cup lemon juice

3 egg yolks

1 whole egg

3 tablespoons unsalted butter

MERINGUE:

6 to 7 egg whites

⅛ teaspoon cream of tartar

1 cup sugar

Chocolate Mousse

This mousse is very light—I always get images of those puffy white clouds (cumulus?) in the sky when I cut into it. We fill pie shells and cakes with this mousse, or dip cookies and strawberries into it.

¼ cup water

½ cup sugar

2 cups heavy cream

5 egg yolks

1 whole egg

4 ounces bittersweet chocolate, melted and cooled

2 ounces unsweetened chocolate, melted and cooled

To make a simple syrup, simmer ¼ cup water with ½ cup sugar until it is clear, approximately 4 minutes. Cover and remove from heat. Set aside.

With an electric mixer, whip the cream to soft-peak stage. Cover and refrigerate until you are ready to use it.

In a medium-sized mixing bowl, whip the egg yolks and the whole egg on high speed until light in color and frothy. While they are whipping, reheat the simple syrup to a rolling boil. Whipping on medium speed, gradually add the syrup to the eggs. Pour into a double boiler and, over simmering water, whisk for 5–7 minutes until thick and light in color. Return to the mixer and whip on medium speed for 5 minutes.

Put one-fourth of the melted cooled chocolate into a medium-sized mixing bowl. Add one-fourth of the whipped cream and whisk together briskly with a hand-held wire whisk. Quickly add and whisk in one-fourth of the egg mixture before the chocolate begins to harden. Repeat this process once more. Fold in the remaining ingredients.

Pour the mousse into individual serving cups and chill for two hours before serving. If you are using the mousse for a pie or cake filling, chill for 30 minutes in a bowl covered with plastic wrap, then pour into pie crust or spread on cake.

Yield: Eight to ten ½-cup servings of chocolate mousse (about 5 cups), enough to fill one Chocolate Mousse Cake (p. 36) with two layers of mousse, or one 9-inch pie

SUMMER

—

Sumptuous Summer Fare

BREAKFAST:
Fresh Raspberry Omelet with Orange Blossom Cream Cheese

LUNCH:
Sweet Coconut–Curry Bread with mascarpone and strawberries,
Wild Green Salad with Spiced Nuts, Pear, Montrachet, and Mango

DINNER:
Curried Green Apple Soup with Coriander and Yogurt,
Indian Halibut Cakes with Mango Chutney

SuMMER

—

THE PORCHES AT THE CAFE were made for summer life: in the languorous afternoon hours, patrons linger at their tables enjoying lattes and fresh-baked scones, watching the ferries come and go. Romantic evenings are enhanced by sunsets over Puget Sound and the distant view of Mount Rainier. In the garden the old pear tree is filled with small hard fruit, and the tall, pale hollyhocks make you feel as if you have stepped Mary Poppins-style into a pastel drawing.

Satiated patrons filling the porches are the first sign of everyone's delight in Northwest warmth. But I really know it is summer when I can enjoy a meandering lunch as I walk through the woods, eating berries along the way. We don't have just one or two types of wild berries here. There are salmonberries, salal berries, thimbleberries, blue and red huckleberries, and blackberries, not to mention all of the domesticated berries that we plant in the garden. Should you decide to make a berry-picking excursion, forget about being in a hurry! You have to slow down or you will surely lose or squish half your treasure *and* prick your fingers. So take a deep breath and enjoy the slow, rhythmic sound of sweet morsels plopping into your bucket.

At the cafe, of course, we are smitten by the profusion of berries. We fill omelets with them, topple them over waffles with fresh whipped cream, pocket them inside cakes and pies, toss them into salads, and make savory sauces out of them to pool under seafood—a harmonious marriage of two of the most abundant natural resources of the Northwest. They are a part of every summer meal, along with the cornucopia of produce from small organic farms throughout the region.

Patrons and friends bring their favorite herb or edible flower to the kitchen window, which stays open to the garden all summer. The reason is twofold: we enjoy a full view of the floral symphony playing just a few feet from the sweltering stove, and our cooks can get to know some of the patrons as they wander by and stop to chat. Andrew, a regular patron who is quite a skilled cook and lavishes us with his appreciative attentions, brings us herbs to taste that we never knew existed, such as the delicious red flower of the honeydew melon sage, whose nectar actually tastes like the sweet melon it is named after. Andrew's bags of specialty herbs create lovely excursions in flavor for our weekend brunches and evening meals. One day he even showed up with lush, large-leafed marjoram and mother-of-thyme seedlings and planted them himself in our little herb garden out back. Sometimes, it is hard to know who is feeding whom around here.

In addition to the berry-and-herb extravaganza, our summer menus highlight all the fruits of the season in every meal. I use peaches, nectarines, mangos, papayas, kiwis, and more—either raw or cooked as little as possible for the freshest flavor. Salsas, chutneys, salads, chilled soups, risottos, omelets, coffee cakes, muffins, pies, waffles: whatever we offer seems to beg for the sweet touch of ripe summer fruits.

Every meal in the long stretch of summer light seems to carry to the table color, refreshing coolness, and ease. Good conversation, friendship, and leisure fill every corner of the garden, decks, and dining room. Come August, in our languor it is even easy to ignore the shift of the earlier setting sun. The crisp air of fall will arrive soon enough. We might as well enjoy summer while we can.

Fresh Raspberry Omelet with Orange Blossom Cream Cheese

The first time I served this omelet was for our first Mother's Day at the cafe. I wanted something sensuous, fragrant, and beautiful. The bright red of the raspberry purée on top of the yellow egg, with the soft cream cheese inside, is dramatic and delicious. We served the omelets on black plates, garnished with honeydew melon and honeysuckle blossoms.

For the orange blossom cream cheese : With an electric mixer, beat together the cream cheese, orange zest and juice, orange-flower water, and sugar or honey until smooth and creamy. Set aside.

For the raspberry purée: In a food processor or blender, purée the raspberries, sugar, and lemon zest and juice until smooth and bright in color.

For the omelets: For each omelet, heat 1½ teaspoons of butter or oil on medium heat in a large omelet pan. Beat 3 of the eggs, and pour into the pan, making sure they spread out to the edges. Cook until the edges of the eggs are done and you can flip the omelet. Remove from heat immediately. Cover half of the omelet with ½ cup of the orange blossom cream cheese and ½ cup of fresh raspberries. Fold over the omelet to cover the filling. Repeat this process for the other three omelets, keeping each one warm (you can cover each with a plate) as it is cooked. Top each omelet with raspberry purée and serve immediately.

Yield: 4 servings

ORANGE BLOSSOM CREAM CHEESE:

1 pound cream cheese, at room temperature

Zest of 1 orange

⅓ cup freshly squeezed orange juice

1 tablespoon orange-flower water

4 teaspoons sugar or honey

RASPBERRY PURÉE:

2 cups fresh raspberries

3 tablespoons sugar

Zest and juice of 1 lemon

OMELETS:

6 teaspoons butter or canola oil

12 eggs

2 cups fresh raspberries

Lemony Polenta with Mascarpone and Berries

The first few years the cafe was open, I would wake up early enough to go gather wild huckleberries and wild blackberries or blueberries from my garden, just for the sheer pleasure of experiencing the slowed-down time of meandering through the woods and the sensation of gathering something that was always there for the taking—no ordering, no money changing hands, no middle person, just myself out walking and picking. My favorite berries for this dish are blackberries, I think partly because the black against the yellow of the polenta is so dramatic. However, raspberries, blueberries, and huckleberries are just as delicious.

---

6 cups milk

2 cups raw polenta

Zest of 2 lemons

3 tablespoons butter

½ cup honey

1 teaspoon salt

3 cups fresh berries (blackberries, huckleberries, blueberries, or raspberries)

6 tablespoons mascarpone cheese

In a large, heavy-bottomed soup pot, bring the milk to a simmer. Add the polenta, stirring constantly until the polenta begins to bubble. Turn to low heat and continue cooking, stirring occasionally, for another 15 minutes. Stir in the lemon zest, butter, honey, and salt.

For each serving, put 1 cup of the polenta into a bowl and top it with ½ cup berries and 1 tablespoon mascarpone.

Yield: 6 servings

SUMMER SOLSTICE MIMOSA

Victoria came to cook and help run the cafe when I was in the throes of compiling and refining recipes for this book. She had sold her restaurant in Australia and wanted to be near family who happened to be living in Kingston. Lucky me! She brought many fantastic recipes and ideas and general professional good sense to the cafe. One of her favorite drinks that she introduced to us is this mimosa. It really is dangerous—because it is so good.

2 tablespoons Peachtree schnapps

½ cup orange juice

⅔ cup champagne

1 honeysuckle flower for garnish

Stir the schnapps, orange juice, and champagne in a glass. Top with the honeysuckle flower!

Yield: 1 mimosa (about 10 ounces)

Indian Halibut Cakes

These cakes are light and aromatic. I always serve them with a fruit chutney, such as Mango Chutney (p. 138). The herbs and spices in the cakes and those in the chutney belong together. These are a cafe favorite for breakfast, lunch, or dinner.

Bake halibut at 350°F for 20 minutes, or until fish will flake. Cool and flake. You should have about 5 cups.

In a medium-sized mixing bowl, combine the fish and all of the other ingredients except the oil, and mix well. Make into 12 cakes and refrigerate until ready to fry.

Lightly coat a nonstick skillet with the oil. When it is hot, fry the cakes until they are golden brown on both sides. Serve immediately with Mango Chutney.

Yield: 6 servings (12 cakes)

2 pounds fresh boneless halibut fillets

2 tablespoons peeled and minced fresh gingerroot

1 tablespoon minced garlic

¾ cup minced fresh cilantro

Zest of 2 lemons

4 teaspoons curry powder

1½ teaspoons garam masala

2 eggs

1½ cups dry bread crumbs

1 cup mayonnaise

1½ cups minced onion

2 teaspoons salt

Canola oil for frying

Mango Chutney (p. 138)

Sourdough Waffles with Fresh Berries

*My good friend Peggy gave me a 100-year-old sourdough starter when I started
the cafe. I call it "Grandmother" and tend it with devoted care in hopes it'll live forever.
At the cafe we make all of our own sandwich bread, sourdough being only one kind. We all vie
for the chewy hot crusts when the bread comes out of the oven. These waffles are my
favorite for the same reason: they're a little chewy, with a light crust.*

*There is nothing better than a sourdough waffle with fresh berries of any kind
in the summer. If you are feeling a little more decadent, whip up some fresh cream
with a little lemon zest and a pinch of sugar to top it off.*

*When using sourdough starter, you must "feed" it the night before you
plan to bake. The resulting mixture is called the "sponge."*

---

2 cups water or nonfat milk

2½ cups flour

1 cup sourdough starter (see Note)

4 tablespoons oil

¾ cup milk

1 egg

2 tablespoons honey

1 teaspoon salt

1 teaspoon baking soda

⅔ cup flour

2½ cups fresh berries (raspberries, blackberries, or blueberries)

To make a sponge from the sourdough starter, begin the night before. Whisk the 2 cups of water or milk and the 2½ cups of flour into the sourdough starter. Let sit overnight.

The next morning, whisk into the sponge the oil, the ¾ cup of milk, the egg, and the honey.

Sift together the salt, baking soda, and the ⅔ cup of flour and whisk into the batter.

Heat and grease the waffle iron. Pour ¾ cup batter for each waffle onto the waffle iron and cook for about 3 minutes.

Top with fresh whole berries and real maple syrup.

Note: Any store with specialty food sections should have a starter "dry mix" to which you just add water.

Yield: Five 7-inch waffles

Sweet Coconut–Curry Bread

This is one of my favorite summer breads. I serve it for weekend brunches with mascarpone and thinly sliced strawberries on top. Add soft scrambled eggs with chives, a hot foamy latte, and the view of Mount Rainier, and one might loll languorously all day in the garden.

In a medium-sized bowl, mix the yeast with the warm water and sugar or honey. Let sit until it becomes bubbly, about 3 minutes.

Preheat oven to 350°F.

Whisk in the oil, eggs, salt, curry powder, and coconut, in that order. Whisk in 1 cup of flour until the dough looks elastic and spongy. Keep adding the flour, ½ cup at a time, until you can no longer whisk the mixture. Turn the dough onto a floured flat surface and knead in the rest of the flour, ½ cup at a time, until the dough does not stick to the kneading surface. Turn into an oiled bowl, cover, and let rise until it doubles in size. Knead into a baguette shape and place on a lightly oiled 9 x 17-inch baking sheet. Cover and let rise again for ½ hour. Bake for 25–30 minutes until golden brown on top.

1 envelope (1 tablespoon) active dry yeast
1 cup warm water
½ cup sugar or honey
⅓ cup canola oil
2 eggs
1¾ teaspoons salt
1¾ teaspoons curry powder
1⅓ cups unsweetened flaked coconut
3 cups unbleached white flour plus additional as needed

Yield: 1 loaf

Carrot Poppyseed Apricot Bread

*One morning our day cook Stephanie came in and said she had tasted
a carrot, poppyseed, and apricot bread that she thought would make a nice
brunch item. I just happened to be working on brunch specials for the weekend,
so I decided to try my own variation. Sliced, griddled, and served with
Hazelnut Butter (p. 49), it also makes a divine French toast.*

1 envelope (1 tablespoon) active dry yeast

½ cup honey

1 cup warm water

1 egg

1 teaspoon orange zest

⅓ cup canola oil

2 teaspoons salt

⅔ cup grated carrots

⅓ cup poppyseeds

⅔ cup dried apricots, thinly sliced

4 cups flour plus additional as needed

In a medium-sized bowl, mix the yeast with the honey and water. Let it sit until it bubbles, about 3 minutes.

Preheat oven to 350°F.

Whisk the egg, orange zest, canola oil, and salt into the yeast mixture until fully incorporated. Stir in the carrots, poppyseeds, and apricots. Stir in 1 cup of flour at a time until the dough becomes too stiff to stir. Turn the dough onto a floured flat surface and knead in the rest of the flour, ½ cup at a time, until the dough does not stick to the kneading surface. Turn into an oiled bowl, cover, and let rise until it doubles in size. Knead, form into a baguette shape, and place on an oiled 9 x 17-inch baking sheet. Cover and let rise again for ½ hour. Bake for 25–30 minutes until golden brown on top.

Yield: 1 loaf

Summer Fruit Gazpacho

In making fruit soups, it is important to use ripe fruit. The amount of spice and sweetener needed can vary a great deal depending on how much natural sugar is in the fruit. This particular soup is delicious either hot or cold. I garnish it with a good plain yogurt, sometimes adding to the yogurt a bit of orange zest and orange-flower water.

In a medium-sized soup pot, bring the water, apple juice, sugar, cinnamon stick, and gingerroot to a boil. Remove from heat and cool in the refrigerator. When the stock is cool, add the fruits, cilantro, lime zest and juice, cayenne, and salt. Cover and chill for 1 hour. Garnish each serving with 1 tablespoon of yogurt.

Yield: 6–8 servings

2 cups water
2 cups apple juice
⅔ cup sugar
1 cinnamon stick
1½ tablespoons peeled and minced fresh gingerroot
1½ cups minced cantaloupe
1½ cups minced mango
2 cups minced pineapple
¾ cup chopped sweet seedless red grapes
1 cup whole fresh tart berries (I like blackberries)
⅔ cup cilantro leaves
Zest and juice of 2 limes
¼ teaspoon cayenne
½ teaspoon salt
½ cup plain yogurt for garnish

Curried Green Apple Soup with Coriander and Yogurt

The first time I tasted the combination of ingredients in this soup was at my sister B. Sue's house. The flavor is a little tart, with a hint of spice and natural fruit sweetness. The combination of hot ginger, garlic, and red pepper flakes with cool yogurt, lemon zest, and other sweet spices makes for a harmonious balance of sweet, not-too-hot, and sensuous.

2 tablespoons minced garlic

2 tablespoons peeled and grated fresh gingerroot

1 cup diced onion

2 large Granny Smith apples, peeled, cored, and quartered

4 tablespoons butter or canola oil

1½ cups apple juice

1½ teaspoons whole coriander seed

¼ teaspoon whole cumin seed

Zest and juice of 1 lemon

½ teaspoon ground cinnamon

¼ teaspoon ground allspice

½ teaspoon ground cardamom

¼ teaspoon red pepper flakes

1⅛ teaspoons salt

2 tablespoons sugar

1 cup plain yogurt

In a medium-sized, heavy-bottomed soup pot, sauté the garlic, gingerroot, onion, and apples in the butter or oil until the onion becomes transparent. Add the apple juice, cover, and bring to a boil. Turn down to simmer for 25 minutes or until the apple is completely broken down.

While the soup is simmering, toast the coriander and cumin seed on high heat in a heavy-bottomed dry skillet, stirring continuously, until golden. Grind to a powder with a mortar and pestle or in a coffee or spice grinder. Add to the soup along with the lemon zest and juice, cinnamon, allspice, cardamom, red pepper flakes, salt, sugar, and yogurt. Turn soup off. Serve immediately.

Yield: 4–6 servings

Tomato Soup with Coriander and Cinnamon

*Although I have tasted Campbell's tomato soup only once or twice, every time
I make this soup its color conjures up memories of that traditional staple from the '50s
and '60s. However, the smells and flavors in this tomato soup are from another world.*

*This is a light tomato soup, best made when the tomatoes are truly ripe and just off the vine.
It has a sweet fragrance because of the cinnamon. I serve it with a plain yogurt garnish.*

In a 3-quart pot, melt the butter or oil and sauté the onion, tomatoes, and potatoes, adding them to the pot in that order. Add the water and bring to a boil. Turn to low heat, cover, and simmer for 25 minutes. Meanwhile, in a small, dry skillet over high heat, toast the coriander seed until light brown. Grind it to a powder with a mortar and pestle or in a small coffee or spice grinder. Add the coriander, cinnamon, nutmeg, cloves, and orange zest and juice to the tomato mixture. Blend in a food processor until smooth. Put the soup back in the pot and return to low heat. Add the salt, sugar or honey, and cream. Heat gently but do not boil. Serve immediately.

Yield: 4 servings

4 tablespoons butter or oil

2 cups diced onion

5 cups diced fresh Roma tomatoes

2 cups peeled and diced potatoes

2 cups water

1 tablespoon whole coriander seed

1½ teaspoons cinnamon

1 teaspoon nutmeg

½ teaspoon cloves

Zest and juice of 1 orange

1 tablespoon salt

2 tablespoons sugar or honey

1 cup heavy cream

Chilled Peach Soup with Gingerroot and White Wine

Chilled fruit soups embody the sweetness of summer. After tiring of the more traditional gazpacho or vichyssoise, I started experimenting with fruits as a soup base. This particular recipe is a good starting point for many fruit soups. You can substitute nectarines, strawberries, mango, or papaya for the peaches, and with a little adjustment for sweetness (because fruit varies so much in sugar content), you will always end up with a delicious summer soup. In general, add 1 teaspoon of sweetener at a time, to taste. I garnish this soup with Summer Strawberry Salsa (p. 143), both for color and for a spicy balance to the sweet flavor.

---

4 cups skinned and diced peaches

1 teaspoon peeled and minced fresh gingerroot

⅛ teaspoon cayenne

Zest and juice of 2 limes

1 cup nonfat yogurt

¼ cup muscat canelli

¼ teaspoon salt

¼ teaspoon freshly grated nutmeg

1 tablespoon honey or sugar

Summer Strawberry Salsa (p. 143)

In a blender or food processor, purée the peaches until smooth. Pour into a bowl and whisk in the gingerroot, cayenne, lime zest and juice, yogurt, wine, salt, nutmeg, and honey or sugar. Taste and adjust sweetness if needed. Chill for 1 hour and serve, garnished with Summer Strawberry Salsa.

Storage: This soup will keep in a tightly lidded container in the refrigerator for up to 2 days.

Note: If this soup seems a little thick, you can add a little apple juice, a few tablespoons at a time, to thin it.

Yield: 4 servings

Hot Summer Blueberry Soup

I am honored to have my two nieces, Gesche and Britte, come to stay with me in summer for various bits of time. They are both great help in the cafe, having grown up with our familial love of food and the preparation thereof. The very first time they were here and our blueberries were in full harvest, I realized I had lucked out. Somewhere in dreamland, before I had even come to full consciousness, I heard laughter and banter along with the rhythmic "kerplunk" of the berries into the bucket. Sad to say, since the cafe opened I myself have been too short on time to fully harvest the blueberries.

Although I make many chilled fruit soups in the summer, I decided I wanted to experiment with a hot soup. This one is somewhat Thai in flavor because of the coconut milk, lime, and kaffir lime leaves. I garnish it with a good plain yogurt to balance the hot, sweet flavor.

In a medium-sized, heavy-bottomed pot, whisk together the coconut milk, apple juice, lime zest and juice, cornstarch, and sugar until the cornstarch is dissolved. Turn on heat to medium-high, add the blueberries, and stir constantly until the mixture comes to a boil. Turn to low, continue stirring, and add the gingerroot, garlic, salt, lime leaf, and cayenne pepper. Continue cooking for another 3–5 minutes. Turn off and serve immediately, garnished with plain yogurt and cilantro leaves.

Yield: 6 servings

2 cups unsweetened coconut milk

1 cup apple juice

1 tablespoon minced lime zest

⅓ cup freshly squeezed lime juice

5 teaspoons cornstarch

5 tablespoons sugar

4 cups blueberries

2 tablespoons peeled and minced fresh gingerroot

1 teaspoon minced garlic

½ teaspoon salt

1 kaffir lime leaf, minced

⅛ teaspoon cayenne pepper

6 tablespoons plain yogurt for garnish

Cilantro leaves for garnish

Braided Salmon and Halibut with Brandied Wild Blackberry Sauce

At the cafe I get mostly whole fish. I am always asking for "a halibut and a salmon that are the same length, please" so that I can braid the fish. I always get a little silence at the other end of the phone when I ask for this favor. Although braided fish may sound strange, the effect is stunning on the plate.

In the beginning I pretended I was 13 again, with my sisters, taking turns braiding our waist-length straight-as-an-arrow hair into 30 little braids to make it frizzy. Somehow it made the idea of braiding fish seem simple. It really is. Once you get the hang of it.

---

1 pound salmon fillet, in one piece

½ pound halibut fillet, the same length as the salmon fillet, in one piece

4 cups blackberries

1 cup late harvest riesling

4 teaspoons minced fresh rosemary

Zest of 1 lemon

2 tablespoons freshly squeezed lemon juice

1 tablespoon cornstarch

¼ cup sugar

6 tablespoons brandy

⅔ cup dry white wine

Lay the fish fillets flat on your work surface. With a very sharp fillet knife, slice thin ropes, approximately ¼ inch thick, lengthwise from top to bottom. You need 8 salmon ropes and 4 halibut ropes.

Take 2 salmon ropes and 1 halibut rope. Lay the halibut rope between the two salmon ropes and braid from the top down. Set aside. Repeat three more times to make four braids.

In a medium-sized pot on medium-high heat, bring the blackberries and the riesling to a simmer. Add the rosemary, lemon zest, and lemon juice.

In a small bowl, stir together the cornstarch, sugar, and brandy until the cornstarch is completely dissolved. Add to the simmering blackberries, stirring continuously until the sauce clears. Turn off immediately.

Put the dry white wine in a small skillet and lay the four braids in the wine. Turn the heat to high and cover. As soon as you see steam coming out the sides of the lid, turn to low. Cook approximately 5–8 minutes, checking the fish frequently to make sure it is not overdone. The cooking time will vary depending on the thickness of the ropes.

Pool approximately ⅓ cup of the blackberry sauce on each of four plates. Lay the braids on top of the sauce and serve.

Storage: Any extra blackberry sauce will keep in a tightly lidded container in the refrigerator for 1 week.

Yield: 4 servings

WILD GREEN SALAD WITH SPICED NUTS, PEAR, MONTRACHET, AND MANGO

My friend Rebecca grows over 20 different kinds of delicious herbs, greens, and edible flowers for the cafe. Her mix varies greatly depending on what is burgeoning that day or week, but a typical mix might combine various mustards, bronze fennel, sweet cicely, sorrels, golden purslane, salad burnet, nasturtiums, miner's lettuce, lamb's-quarters, and more! Our cook, Stephanie, loves delivery day because she gets to be the recipient of a beautiful bouquet along with the greens in the wee hours of the morn.

12 ounces mixed seasonal wild greens	½ cup Montrachet cheese
1 cup Spiced Nuts (p. 68)	1 cup sliced mango
1 cup unpeeled sliced pear (Bosc pears are my favorite in winter)	1 cup Fresh Ginger–Curry Vinaigrette (p. 137)

Lightly toss all ingredients together. Serve immediately.

Note: At the cafe we keep the fresh greens as dry as possible, lightly covered with paper towel and cool. They keep well for up to 4 days.

Yield: 4 large servings

Fresh Yellowfin Tuna Cakes

*Rick, my sister Beth's neighbor, fishes off the coast of Washington and Oregon.
Once a year, he showers all of his friends with fresh tuna. He has so much tuna
during the height of the season that he keeps asking me for recipes or ideas so he won't
get tired of eating it. Although fresh tuna needs very little adornment to make
a delicious meal, I decided to create yet one more kind of fish cake.*

2 pounds fresh yellowfin tuna loin

2 tablespoons olive oil

1 clove garlic, peeled and split

Salt and pepper

2 cups minced onion

1½ cups dry bread crumbs

3 tablespoons minced garlic

Zest of 2 lemons

½ teaspoon black pepper

2 cups roughly chopped cilantro

3 eggs, beaten

1½ cups mayonnaise

2 teaspoons salt

Papaya-Mango Salsa (p. 7) or
Pineapple-Lime Salsa (p. 139)

Preheat oven to 375°F.

Rub the tuna loin with olive oil and garlic. Sprinkle with salt and pepper. Wrap in foil and bake for approximately 20–25 minutes, until the fish is tender but cooked through. Cool, flake, and place in a medium-sized mixing bowl.

Add the rest of the ingredients and mix thoroughly until the bread crumbs and eggs are distributed evenly. Make into 10 cakes and refrigerate. At this point you can refrigerate the cakes for up to 24 hours until you are ready to serve them.

Lightly oil a smooth-bottomed skillet. Fry the cakes until they are golden brown on both sides, approximately 2 minutes on each side.

Serve with Papaya-Mango Salsa or Pineapple-Lime Salsa.

Yield: 5 servings (10 cakes)

FISH CAKES

My feelings about perfectly fresh fish, simply prepared, with little augmentation, border on the religious. Years ago I would have scorned any cook who brazenly "ruined" fresh fish with bold spices and other heavy flavorings. Yet now, assertively seasoned little fish cakes that melt in the mouth are the centerpiece for some of my favorite meals.

Why did I start making fish cakes? I order only fresh whole fish, and fillet or steak it myself. This practice began because I wanted to do different types of preparation: sometimes I would bake the fish whole and chill it with dips and sauces, sometimes I would braid it, and sometimes I would steak it. Whatever the preparation, I would always end up with a large (and uncouth, according to the vegetarians on our crew) fish skeleton with a lot of meat still on it. I couldn't throw it away. So I decided to rub it down, head and all, in olive oil, garlic, and a little salt and pepper, wrap it in foil, and bake it. If nothing else, I could make omelets or quiche out of it, or toss it into some fish stew. The first time I had the remains of a fish baking, I was simultaneously acting out one of my predictable rituals—leafing through the index of a cookbook to get inspired. Under "F" in *The New Basics Cookbook* (Sheila Lukins & Julee Rosso), I saw "fish cake," and turned to the page to see what exactly they were talking about. The recipe was an unconventional mix of cod fish, curry, and coconut, served with pineapple salsa. I was hooked.

I make fish cakes out of almost any fish or shellfish—salmon, halibut, oysters, shrimp, tuna, scallops, to name a few. I enjoy creating thematic preparations. For instance, one day I had some halibut and I thought a Mexican chile and oregano flavoring would be good, served with a fruit salsa. Another time I had some salmon and wanted an East Indian flavoring, so I flavored the cakes with curry and served them with Mango Chutney (p. 138). Another favorite is an aromatic Middle Eastern combination of cinnamon, currants, and pine nuts mixed with salmon or halibut. Almost any cakes you make can follow the same basic mixture: prebaked fish, bread crumbs, onions, eggs, zest, and some type of oil (sesame, canola, or olive), or even homemade aioli or mayonnaise to double as an egg-and-oil mixture. Because the cakes are mixed and shaped beforehand, they are an easy meal to serve when you have guests. I have served them for breakfast with soft scrambled eggs, for brunch with a wild green salad, and for dinner with rice and Dilled Cucumber Salad (p. 137). And I always serve them with some condiment, whether it be a raita, a salsa, or chutney.

Summer Ricotta Ravioli in Curried Peach Sauce

*I keep thinking of other ways to use this sauce, but the simplicity
of the ricotta with curried peach is truly perfect.*

2 cups ricotta cheese

16 ravioli squares (see Ravioli Dough, p. 73)

5 cups peeled and cubed peaches

Zest of 2 lemons

½ cup and 2 tablespoons freshly squeezed lemon juice

½ cup sugar

¼ cup and 2 tablespoons peeled and minced fresh gingerroot

¼ teaspoon salt

5 teaspoons curry powder

4 tablespoons (½ stick) butter

1 cup apple juice

Place 2 tablespoons of ricotta in the middle of each ravioli. Fold and press the edges. Cover and refrigerate.

In a medium-sized pot on medium-high heat, bring the peaches, lemon zest and juice, and sugar to a low boil. Turn to low heat and cook another 15 minutes. Stir in the gingerroot, salt, curry powder, butter, and apple juice. Cook another 5 minutes. Set aside and keep warm.

Place a large skillet, ¾ full of water on high heat and bring to a boil. Drop in the ravioli, 4 at a time, so that the water keeps boiling. Be sure to keep it at a soft boil so that the movement of the water doesn't break the ravioli. Cook al dente, approximately 8–10 minutes.

Pool ½ cup of the peach sauce on each plate. Place 3 ravioli on top of each and serve.

Storage: Any extra peach sauce will keep in a tightly lidded container in the refrigerator for up to one week.

Yield: 4–5 servings

Grilled Salmon with Miso-Orange-Cilantro Glaze

*Although each of the four main ingredients here has a strong flavor,
together they produce a balanced, mouthwatering dish. With its orange
and cilantro, this summery glaze is refreshing and attractive.*

In a food processor, blend the miso, orange zest and juice, brown sugar, cilantro, and gingerroot to a smooth paste.

Lightly oil a nonstick large skillet on high heat. When the oil is hot, place the salmon fillets in the skillet for 3 minutes. Flip. Brush the tops of the fillets with the glaze and cover, turning to low heat. Cook until the fish just barely flakes apart, approximately 3–5 minutes. Serve.

Storage: Any leftover glaze will keep in a tightly lidded container in the refrigerator for up to 2 weeks.

Note: For people who follow lowfat or nonfat diets, this glaze can also be used with a leaner, white fish or chicken.

Yield: 4 servings

1 cup mellow white miso
Zest and juice of 1 large orange
½ cup brown sugar
½ cup cilantro leaves
1 tablespoon peeled and minced fresh gingerroot
1 teaspoon canola oil
4 salmon fillets, about 5 ounces each

Consummate Crab Cakes

*To me, crab symbolizes the decadent side of Northwest living. Although we have
to put up with gray skies, rain, and long winters, one summer meal with fresh crab as the
centerpiece makes it all worthwhile. Visions of pulling up the crab pots, hauling them home,
putting your largest kettles full of water on to boil, dumping in the crabs, and setting out bowls
of dipping butter are all you really need to feel once again at peace with where you live.*

1 pound cooked crabmeat

¾ cup unsweetened coconut milk

½ teaspoon hot chili oil

1 cup finely chopped green onion

½ cup finely chopped cilantro

1½ tablespoons peeled and minced fresh gingerroot

2 teaspoons minced fresh lemongrass

1 minced kaffir lime leaf

½ cup bread crumbs

2 eggs, beaten

1 teaspoon salt

1 tablespoon sugar

1 tablespoon canola oil

Squeeze the crabmeat as dry as possible. (I use a clean towel and wring it as tightly as I can, until the meat actually looks dry.)

In a medium-sized bowl, mix all of the ingredients together until evenly combined. Shape into 8 equal-sized cakes. At this point you can cover the cakes tightly and refrigerate them overnight.

In a lightly oiled nonstick skillet on medium-high heat, fry the cakes until golden brown, approximately 3 minutes. Flip, and brown the other sides. Serve immediately.

Note: I like to serve these with Dilled Cucumber Salad (following page).

Yield: 4 servings

Fresh Ginger—Curry Vinaigrette

*I use this dressing with Wild Green Salad (p. 131). I have also used it with couscous
or rice salads if they have an Eastern/Asian flavor.*

Put the gingerroot, garlic, curry powder, cinnamon,
and rice vinegar in a blender or food processor.
Blend for 1 minute. Continue blending while
pouring the oil in a fine stream into the vinegar
mixture.

Storage: This dressing will keep in a tightly lidded
container in the refrigerator for up to 1 month.

Yield: About 2 cups

2 tablespoons peeled and minced
fresh gingerroot

1 tablespoon minced garlic

4 teaspoons curry powder

1½ teaspoons cinnamon

¾ cup seasoned rice vinegar

1 cup canola oil

DILLED CUCUMBER SALAD

Sometimes the simplest things to make prove to be the most loved. I have served this
salad on our antipasto platter since we opened. People still ask for "more cucumber
salad, please," when ordering. There are some combinations that please the palate
worldwide—for example, cucumbers and vinegar, the essence of pickles. This non-aged,
fresh-from-the-garden variation on that eternal theme is irresistible.

3 cups cucumber, peeled, cut in half
lengthwise, seeded, and sliced thinly
on a sharp diagonal

¼ cup seasoned rice vinegar

3 tablespoons canola oil

1 tablespoon minced fresh dill,
or 1 teaspoon dried

1 tablespoon minced garlic

½ teaspoon salt

½ teaspoon sugar

In a small mixing bowl toss all ingredients together. Serve.

Storage: This salad will keep in a tightly lidded container in the refrigerator for up to 2
days. After that, it is still good but tastes more like a pickle than a fresh salad.

Yield: 3 cups

Mango Chutney

When I make this chutney, I try to prepare enough for the guaranteed question that comes over the kitchen counter: "Can I buy a pint of that?"

I use this with traditional "rice table" meals, with seafood, poultry, salads, and meats, as a condiment, or in dressings. Just make enough so that you can be generous with it.

---

2 cups peeled and diced fresh mango

Zest of 2 lemons

⅔ cup sugar

¼ cup peeled and minced fresh gingerroot

⅔ cup seasoned rice vinegar

¼ teaspoon red pepper flakes

2 teaspoons minced garlic

In a 2-quart saucepan, bring all of the ingredients to a boil. Turn down to simmer until the liquid becomes syrupy, approximately 25–30 minutes.

Storage: This chutney will keep in a tightly lidded container in the refrigerator for up to 1 month.

Note: For a different but pleasant twist, add ½ teaspoon garam masala.

Yield: About 2½ cups

Pineapple-Lime Salsa

*I serve this salsa with eggs for breakfast, with fish cakes for brunch, with grilled
tuna for dinner, and on soups for lunch and dinner. It is so delicious and versatile that
I wouldn't hesitate to think about it for dessert! People always ask for more.*

Stir together all ingredients in a bowl. Serve immediately. The cilantro wilts and doesn't keep its fresh
flavor long.

Yield: About 2½ cups

2 cups diced fresh pineapple

1 teaspoon minced fresh jalapeño

Zest and juice of 2 limes

½ cup roughly chopped cilantro
leaves

2 tablespoons sugar

1 teaspoon salt

Citrus—Ancho Chile Sauce

The first time I saw the uninhibited use of fruit and chiles together was in Mark Miller's Coyote Cafe Cookbook. For a while I was putting every kind of fruit and chile together, delighting in the combinations. This sauce is one of my favorites. It bursts on your mouth with the unexpected (and thus somewhat unidentifiable) taste of banana, the clean taste of lime, and the heat of the chiles. I have used it for breakfast (over omelets filled with spicy sausage, onion, and cheddar cheese), with lunch burritos filled with chicken, chiles, and cheese, or for dinner with prawns and Mexican rice. It turns any simple dish of eggs, chicken, fish, or tamales into a celebratory meal. I've even seen chile lovers dip their bread into it!

½ cup whole peeled garlic cloves

6–8 ancho chiles (about 1 cup), soaked, seeded, and puréed (see Note, p. 22)

2 cups diced fresh ripe pineapple

1 banana

6 tablespoons sugar

2 tablespoons salt

½ cup apple juice

Zest and juice of 1 orange

Zest and juice of 2 lemons

Zest and juice of 3 limes

2 cups roughly chopped cilantro leaves

Mince the garlic in a food processor. Add the chiles, pineapple, banana, sugar, salt, and apple juice. Blend until smooth. Add the orange, lemon, and lime zest and juice. Fold in the cilantro.

Storage: This sauce will keep in a tightly lidded container in the refrigerator for up to 2 weeks.

Note: When you are making sauces and salsas with fruit, the ripeness of the fruit affects the recipe dramatically. Be prepared to adjust the seasonings to your taste, especially the amounts of lime, sugar, and salt.

Yield: About 5 cups

Orange Blossom Dressing

You can be in front of the fire on a cold wintry evening, dipping Belgian endive into this dressing, and imagine you are on a white sandy beach in the hot sun. We have used this in many different ways at the cafe—for a simple spinach salad with mango or papaya and Spiced Nuts (p.68), with a light beet salad, or even as a garnish for soups (I especially like the flavor combination of butternut squash and orange blossom). For an additional treat, sprinkle some toasted chopped hazelnuts on top!

Whisk all ingredients together.

Storage: This dressing will keep in a tightly lidded container in the refrigerator for up to 2 weeks.

Yield: About 3 cups

2 cups yogurt
Zest and juice of 1 orange
¼ cup canola oil
2 tablespoons orange-flower water
¼ teaspoon salt
2½ tablespoons sugar

Cool As a Cucumber Raita

Although raita is a traditional East Indian condiment, I've played with it a little to make it more widely applicable. I serve it on the side with fish cakes, such as Ahi Tuna Cakes with Green Onion, Sesame, and Ginger (p. 107) or Mexican Fish Cakes (p. 54). It is also appealing, along with chutney, served with the Pakistani Home Fries (p. 88).

1¼ cups peeled, seeded, diced cucumber

1 cup sweetened plain yogurt (Nancy's Honey Yogurt is my favorite)

2 tablespoons finely chopped cilantro leaves

¼ cup finely chopped green onion

1 tablespoon freshly squeezed lime juice

Pinch of salt

Pinch of sugar

Stir all ingredients together in a medium-sized mixing bowl. Serve immediately. This sauce does not hold well.

Yield: About 2 cups

Summer Strawberry Salsa

The Bainbridge Winery, 20 minutes from our cafe on Bainbridge Island, creates a lovely strawberry wine each year. It goes on sale for one day, and for three years in a row I stood in line for hours (with many others) to get a dozen bottles. The concentrated essence of strawberry intoxicates like no other fragrance.

This salsa reminds me of that strawberry wine. It begs to sit on the tongue and languish as long as possible. I use it as a garnish on top of many chilled fruit soups, such as Chilled Peach Soup (p. 128) or Pear-Ginger Soup (p. 97), or even with fish cakes.

In a small mixing bowl, stir all ingredients together until the juices begin to bleed. Serve immediately. This sauce does not keep well.

Yield: About 1½ cups

1½ cups finely chopped strawberries

¼ cup roughly chopped cilantro leaves

1 teaspoon seeded and minced fresh jalapeño

2 teaspoons lime zest

2 tablespoons and 1 teaspoon freshly squeezed lime juice

½ teaspoon salt

4 teaspoons sugar

Orange Blossom Cake with Berries and Lemon Curd

*Having orange-flower water in the kitchen is like having a magic
potion at your command. Its flavor and aroma are intoxicating—and often quite
puzzling to those who taste this cake, because they are so unexpected. You should be
able to find orange-flower water in any shop that carries products imported
from the Middle East. This recipe makes a lovely wedding cake.*

1 recipe Lemon Curd (recipe follows)

1 recipe Vanilla Buttercream (p. 38)

CAKE:

1¼ cups cake flour, sifted before measuring

1 cup plus ¼ cup sugar

1 tablespoon baking powder

⅜ teaspoon salt

4 egg yolks

½ cup sunflower oil or other light oil

6 tablespoons cold water

Zest of 2 lemons, finely minced

4 tablespoons freshly squeezed lemon juice

3 tablespoons orange-flower water

1 teaspoon lemon or orange extract

6 egg whites

⅛ teaspoon cream of tartar

2 cups firm fresh berries (blueberries or raspberries are our favorites)

Prepare the Lemon Curd and the Vanilla Buttercream.

Preheat oven to 375°F.

Grease three 8-inch cake pans and dust with flour.

Sift the flour, 1 cup of the sugar, the baking powder, and the salt together. Set aside.

In a large mixing bowl, whisk together the egg yolks, oil, water, lemon zest, lemon juice, orange-flower water, and lemon or orange extract. Set aside.

With an electric mixer, whip the egg whites on medium speed until frothy, about 1 minute. Slowly add the cream of tartar and the remaining ¼ cup of sugar while continuing to whip. Turn the mixer to high and whip until the whites form stiff peaks. Set aside.

Gradually sift the sifted dry ingredients over the wet ingredients while folding continuously. When all of the dry ingredients have been incorporated, gently fold the egg whites into the batter.

Divide the batter equally among the three cake pans. Bake at 375°F for 5 minutes. Turn the oven down to 350°F and bake for approximately 15 minutes longer, or until the center of the cake springs back when you touch it. Let cool in the pans for 5 minutes and then invert onto cooling racks.

To assemble the cake: Spread a thin layer of buttercream on the bottom layer. On top of that spread a thin layer of the lemon curd and then a layer of fresh berries. Place the second layer on top of the bottom layer and repeat the process. Place the third layer on top. Ice the top and sides of the cake with the remaining buttercream and chill for about 30 minutes to set.

Note: For an equally delicate variation, try making this cake with rose water instead of orange-flower water.

Yield: One 8-inch three-layered cake

Lemon Curd

*Lemon curd is very versatile. We use it in fruit tarts, lemon mousse,
or cheesecakes—anytime a lemon accent would be nice.*

Put the sugar, butter, and lemon juice into a heavy-bottomed, stainless steel saucepan. Bring the mixture to a boil and remove from the heat.

In a small mixing bowl, whisk the 5 egg yolks and the whole egg. Whisk one third of the hot butter-and-lemon mixture into the eggs and pour back into the pan. Cook slowly, whisking continuously, until the mixture thickens, approximately 5 minutes. Pour into a bowl, cover, and refrigerate for at least 1 hour.

Yield: About 2 cups

¾ cup and 2 tablespoons sugar

12 tablespoons (1½ sticks) unsalted butter

½ cup freshly squeezed lemon juice

5 egg yolks

1 whole egg

Blackberry Pie

*One day an older man came to our back door, his hands full of blackberries
almost the size of your thumb. He informed us that he liked our place and that
he chose two or three restaurants in all the state to sell his own hybrid to.
Without even knowing we were being tested, we had passed!*

*His berry is a family secret. It's called "Dengrin," after his name, Denny Grindall.
His grandchildren help him pick when the berries come on full force about midsummer.
He shows up at our back door with 5-gallon bucketfuls, and our entire kitchen crew becomes
a chain gang of plastic bags, ties, and dark-stained fingers. (Denny insists that whatever
berries we're not going to use that day go in the freezer immediately to keep their fresh flavor.)
Jeannie, our baker, says he is the guardian angel of blackberries. We take as many as he
can give us, for the season disappears all too soon. I try to save just enough so that I can
make a Dengrin blackberry pie for Christmas—there is nothing quite like it, and the taste
of summer in the middle of winter is the best gift I can imagine around the holidays.*

---

1 recipe Basic Pie Crust (p. 148)

6 cups blackberries

2 tablespoons cornstarch

2 tablespoons cake flour

¾ cup brown sugar

6 tablespoons white sugar

¼ teaspoon salt

2 tablespoons freshly squeezed
lemon juice

2 tablespoons unsalted butter

Preheat oven to 425°F.

Prepare Basic Pie Crust and line a 9-inch pie pan, reserving some dough for the top crust. Chill reserved dough.

In a large mixing bowl, combine all of the filling ingredients except the butter. Pour into the pastry-lined pie pan. Dot the top of the fruit with the butter.

Roll out the top crust. Wet the rim of the bottom crust with ice water and place the top crust over the berries. Turn the edges under and crimp. Make little slits in the top of the crust to allow steam to escape while baking.

Place the pie in the center of a piece of tin foil and fold it over the top crust to prevent the edge from browning too fast. Place the pie on a cookie sheet to catch the juices that bubble over.

Bake at 425°F for 10 minutes. Turn the oven down to 350°F and bake for about 45 minutes. Uncover the foil from the edges of the pie, then bake another 30 minutes.

The top crust will be golden brown, and the juices will be thick and bubbling out the top.

Note: You can substitute any other tart, juicy berry for the blackberries in this pie.

Yield: One 9-inch pie

TONYA'S TERRIFIC TRUFFLE ESPRESSO

Tonya is our Sunday barista. She brings her passion for good coffee to the cafe, and we all benefit. Her creations are not just a good Northwest latte. They are an experience. Instead of putting regular ice cubes in our iced lattes, she makes coffee ice cubes so that the coffee will not get watered down. She makes her whipped creams with spices and chocolates. She buys specialty syrups and concocts combinations of flavors that titillate the tongue, topping them with vanilla or raspberry sprinkles or a swirl of semi-sweet chocolate syrup. When we all feel like we are just about dying in the kitchen from the weekend onslaught of customers, Tonya picks our spirits back up with, "Would any of you like a coffee?" I don't even give her an order; I just say, "Whatever your latest experiment is, I'll take it!"

2 shots espresso
4 tablespoons chocolate syrup
1 tablespoon blackberry syrup
1 cup whole milk

3–4 coffee ice cubes (freeze half coffee and half water in an ice tray)
Freshly whipped cream

Mix the 2 shots of espresso with the chocolate and blackberry syrups and let cool for one minute. Add the milk and let cool for another minute. Add the coffee ice cubes, top with whipped cream, and garnish with a drizzle of blackberry syrup. Enjoy!

Yield: One 12-ounce drink

Basic Pie Crust

Everyone who bakes has his or her own passionate "absolutes" about pie crust.
How to make it flaky; how thick or thin it should be (although there is an old tradition,
still tightly adhered to, that the thinner the better—probably because the better the dough,
the harder it is to work, so really, it is all a test in patience); how to make the perfect "crimp";
and whether it should be a little sweet or not sweet at all. If I had to choose one rule that
seemed the most important to me, I would have to say that making pie crust is the surest way
to get good at it. Any recipe you follow will give you the generally agreed upon basics: Handle
as little as possible (Jeannie, our baker, even says it should never be touched by human hands!);
be sure the butter and shortening are cold; keep the pie crust cold at all times; use as little
water as possible. But no recipe is as good as experience—and lots of it. I hate to sound
mysterious, because it really isn't, but experiencing how the dough looks, how it rolls
out (or falls apart), how it crimps and bakes, and then connecting all of that to what
the flavor and texture are like after you've baked it, will be your best guarantee of
making good pie crust. Just say yes. Make a lot of pies. You'll make a lot of friends.

---

1 cup and 2 tablespoons pastry flour

¾ cup unbleached white flour

2 teaspoons sugar

½ teaspoon salt

4 tablespoons (½ stick) unsalted butter, chilled

2 tablespoons vegetable shortening, frozen

4–5 tablespoons ice water

½ teaspoon white vinegar

In a medium-sized mixing bowl, blend the dry ingredients with a hand-held pastry blender. Cut the cold butter and shortening into tablespoon-sized pieces and add to the dry ingredients. With the pastry blender, cut the fats into the flour mixture until they are about the size of small peas. Add the vinegar to the ice water. While stirring the dry mixture with a fork, add half the liquid in a thin, steady stream. Push together some of the dough to see if it will hold together when you let go. If it won't, add more water a dribble at a time just until it will. It should feel moist but not wet.

Yield: Two 9-inch crusts

INDEX

D – E

Photo: Linda Wolf

ABOUT THE AUTHOR

A creative and improvisational cook, Judith Weinstock was a partner in two collective restaurants before joining the Streamliner Diner on Bainbridge Island, Washington. Her innate sense of how foods and seasonings go together was instrumental in the success of that restaurant and its popular namesake cookbook. After selling the diner, she and her family moved to Indianola, Washington. It was while walking one day in neighboring Kingston that she spotted the Kingston Hotel, a vintage building with multiple decks and a view of Puget Sound and the Cascades. Even as her husband was saying, "Judith, you said never again," she was planning her next venture, the Kingston Hotel Cafe.

Judith is committed to organic foods and small-farm production: The cafe gets its chickens from a local farm, its greens from a woman on Bainbridge Island, organic lamb from down the street, basil from a nearby herb farm, and smoked goods from The Kingston Smokehouse. Likewise, the cafe has become a focal point for the community, which helped to create it and continues to help it grow. Heronswood Nursery assisted in reconstructing the entire garden area, while local gardeners and florists regularly contribute additional vegetables and decor. A resident potter has hand-thrown many of the cafe's dishes, and carpenters and young laborers helped restore the building. Various customers regularly bring in firewood, fix the plumbing, and help with big events. Twice a week, area musicians play live music that softly echoes over the quiet ferry landing.

Judith lives with her husband, David, and two children, Devin and Sam.